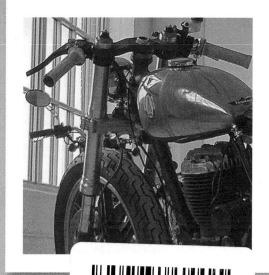

T0386519

BRITISH
CUSTOM MOTORCYCLES

The Brit Chop –
choppers, cruisers,
bobbers & trikes

www.veloce.co.uk

For post publication news, updates and amendments relating to this book please visit www.veloce.co.uk/books/V4621

First published in March 2014 by Veloce Publishing Limited, Veloce House, Parkway Farm Business Park, Middle Farm Way, Poundbury, Dorchester, Dorset, DT1 3AR, England.
Fax 01305 250479/e-mail info@veloce.co.uk/web www.veloce.co.uk or www.velocebooks.com.

ISBN: 978-1-845846-21-3 UPC: 6-36847-04621-7

British Library Cataloguing in Publication Data   A catalogue record for this book is available from the British Library.
Typesetting, design and page make-up all by Veloce Publishing Ltd on Apple Mac. Printed in India by Replika Press.

BRITISH
CUSTOM MOTORCYCLES

*The Brit Chop -
choppers, cruisers,
bobbers & trikes*

Uli Cloesen

Contents

Foreword

My appreciation for British bikes began during my teens, when I saw a Norton Commando overtaking my parent's car on a German motorway; it left quite an impression on me. In the years since I've sampled some T140 Triumphs and Hinckley Bonnevilles, and, in early 2000, while travelling in India, the sight of Royal Enfield Bullets roaming the streets intrigued me greatly. That a British design from the mid-50s was still being made in the twenty-first century, and virtually unchanged, was a rather wonderful experience.

I soon developed a great affection for the Bullet, and this led to me shipping a 350cc Bullet from India to NZ for some 'Bulleteering' on home ground.

Because most custom bike books these days rarely have more than one or two Triumph customs (usually lost in an ocean of Harley offerings), plus the fact that there's been a noticeable rise in interest for customized parallel twins, I felt that a celebration of all things British – chopper, cruiser, bobber and trike – was in order.

So, what more is there to say? Let the Brit engines shine!

Uli Cloesen

Introduction

Life would be boring without a touch of individuality, creativity and flair. This is especially true when it comes to the world of two- or three-wheeled modes of transport. There has to be an emotional response, a feel good trigger that engages us to build, ride or drive.

So, what triggered the invention of the bobber? When United States soldiers returned home after World War II, they wanted bikes more like those they'd seen in Europe; motorcycles with less bulk than the homegrown machines in the States.

A bobber was created by 'bobbing' or shedding weight, particularly scrapping the front mudguard and shortening the rear one, with the intention of making the bike lighter and faster. A more minimalist ride was perceived to look better than the standard machines. (Note that not all countries allow the removal of mudguards on bikes.)

It wasn't until 1969, when the American road movie *Easy Rider*, starring Peter Fonda, Dennis Hopper and Jack Nicholson appeared, that the term 'chopper' arrived on the scene. Motorcycle enthusiasts found a new way of modifying their bikes, and started changing the angle of the front fork, reducing the size of the fuel tank, and adding 'ape hanger' handlebars to their bikes. To complete the package, a thin front wheel and a large rear tyre were added.

The main difference between bobbers and choppers is that the former are usually built around standard frames, while chopper frames are often cut and welded to suit. Bobbers also often lack chromed parts and long forks.

Cruisers is the term for bikes that copy the style of American machines like Harley or Indian. This segment of the motorcycle market is most popular in the United States. The Big Four bike manufacturers – Honda, Kawasaki, Suzuki and Yamaha – all produced V-twin cruisers for this very important market.

Riding a cruiser typically entails a feet forward riding position, with an upright body. The low-slung design of this type of bike limits its cornering ability. Chopper motorcycles are considered cruisers in this context.

A trike is basically a three-wheeled motorcycle, carrying its rider and up to two passengers depending on specifications. If you like the idea, acceleration and speed of riding a bike, but prefer the safety of an additional wheel, this might be the one for you. In many countries you don't have to wear a helmet riding a trike, because they can be registered like a car.

ACKNOWLEDGEMENTS

The author and publisher wish to acknowledge their debt to all who loaned material and photographs for this book.

You're welcome to contact us to have your British-powered chopper, cruiser, bobber or trike considered for an updated version of this book in the future.

CHAPTER 1
AJS-Hesketh

AJS

AJS was founded by AJ Stevens & Co Ltd in Wolverhampton, England. From its foundation in 1909 to encountering financial trouble in 1931, the company amassed 117 motorcycle world records. After the business was sold, the name continued to be used by Matchless and Norton-Villiers on four-stroke motorcycles until 1969, and, since the name's resale in 1974, on lightweight, two-stroke scramblers. Today, the AJS name continues on small-capacity roadsters and cruisers.

Right & below: Brian from British Iron Works in the UK contributed these images of a friend's AJS chop prior to its sale.

Above: This bobbed AJS was spotted at the Stafford Classic Bike Show in October 2010. It's got a lovely blue/white paint-job. (Courtesy Hazel Clarke)

This 500cc AJS 18 (with rigid frame) from 1946 was originally almost identical to the Matchless G80, and was manufactured in the same AMC factory in London from 1945 to 1966. Both bikes signalled the end of the era of big British singles, once the merger of AMC with Norton took place and production concentrated on twins.

The bike is Austrian-registered, apparently running well, with a super sound and performance, and has a proper working electrical system (the alternator was changed to 12V, but the ignition still has the magneto).

The engine is a 498cc single-cylinder, pushrod, two-valve, four-stroke, the headlight and speedo with trip odometer are Smith originals, and the long fork was professionally converted in the '90s. Frame number 9476, engine number 46/182030. (Courtesy www.italo-classics.at)

ARIEL

Ariel Motorcycles was based in Birmingham. The original company was established in 1870 by James Starley and William Hillman to make bicycles. In 1896, the company merged with Westwood Manufacturing, and made a powered tricycle in 1898, with a de Dion engine. Later, Ariel merged with a company called Components Ltd, but this venture failed and, in 1930, Ariel regained control and set up a new factory in Birmingham.

In 1944, the company was sold to BSA, but production lasted only until 1963 when BSA closed the factory and moved production to Small Heath. Ariel produced its last motorcycle in 1967.

Morgan Ariel Special. (Courtesy John Bartram)

A Components tricycle with a de Dion Bouton engine behind the rear axle. Top speed was 20mph; capacity 239cc.
(Courtesy Paul McCurley)

The Muriel three-wheeler (top right) is another approach to triking, this time by John Bradshaw in the UK.

John wrote the book *Transmogrification* about his build: "With inspiration and help from friends in the Morgan and Ariel worlds – plus many others – a three-wheeler has been built in the vintage style, out of many parts, mainly from Morgans, Urals and Ariels, hence its name: Muriel. Some bits even came from ancient aircraft, so its Aero label is almost justified." www.jrbpub.net/books/transmogrification

The Ariel Square Four was conceived in 1928 by Edward Turner. His pair of across-the-frame parallel twins, linked by a pair of gears, created a very compact engine. Originally in 500cc guise, capacity increased to 600cc in 1932, and, in 1937, a 1000cc version came onto the market. The Square Four was the biggest British bike on the market after Vincent closed its doors in 1955. Production ceased in 1958.

A 1956 Square Four at the Gilmore Car Museum Antique Motorcycle Show in Hickory Corners, Michigan. (Courtesy Pete Walsh)

Square Fours lend themselves to excellent-looking customs, as this Ariel bobber shows.

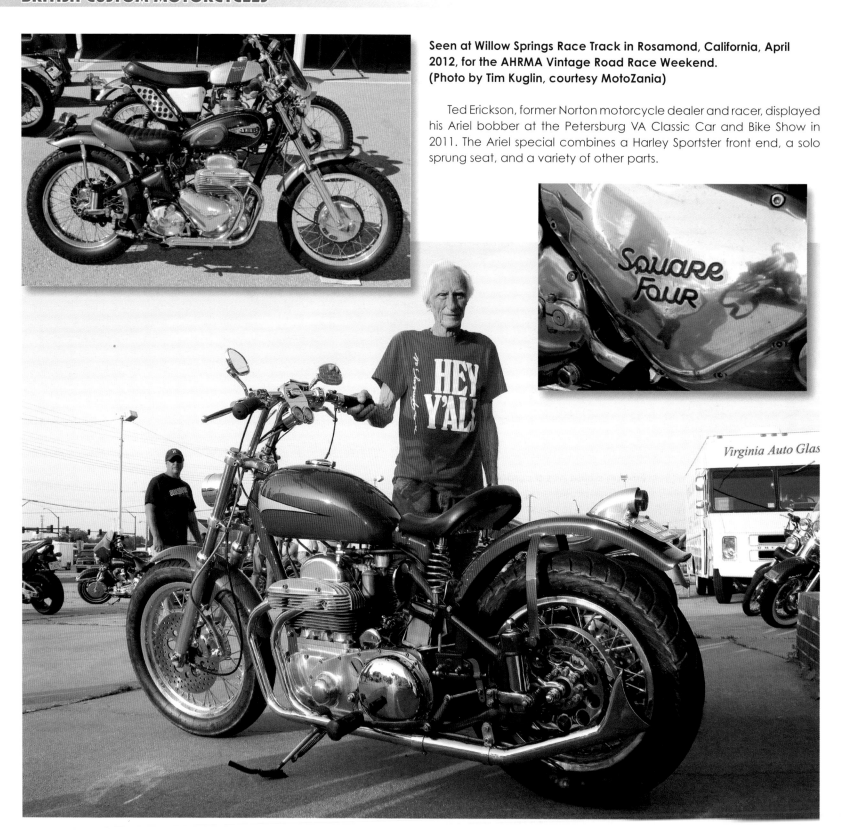

Seen at Willow Springs Race Track in Rosamond, California, April 2012, for the AHRMA Vintage Road Race Weekend. (Photo by Tim Kuglin, courtesy MotoZania)

Ted Erickson, former Norton motorcycle dealer and racer, displayed his Ariel bobber at the Petersburg VA Classic Car and Bike Show in 2011. The Ariel special combines a Harley Sportster front end, a solo sprung seat, and a variety of other parts.

Opposite, above & below: Ted Erikson's bike has a purposeful stance, and the 997cc four-cylinder, ohv four-stroke produces 42bhp at 5800rpm. (Courtesy Tom Saunders)

BROUGH SUPERIOR

Brough Superiors were made by George Brough in Haydn Road, Nottingham, England, from 1919 to 1940. Approximately 3048 machines were made in a 21-year production run, with an estimated one third still in existence.

Above and overleaf, top: Brough Superior SS120 photographed at the Goodwood Festival of Speed in July 2011. (Courtesy Andrew Wright)

Left: On display at the London International Custom Show in 2010, Alexandra Palace in north London, with different forks. (Courtesy Ray Douglas)

Lawrence of Arabia (TE Lawrence) became known as the most ardent fan of the marque, owning seven Broughs.

One of its models, the SS100 (Super Sports), powered by JAP (JA Prestwich) or Matchless 1000cc overhead valve V-twin engines, was built from 1924 to 1940.

This Brough Superior SS120 version above was built by the late Alec Card in the '90s. Card owned the company for a number of years, and this is the last one made in Britain.

Mark Upham runs restoration firm British Only Austria in Pettenbach, and bought the Brough trademark and assets from Bonhams in 2008. Acting on behalf of Netherton Industries, Upham reorganized Brough Superior Motorcycles, with the revitalized firm now manufacturing and selling Brough Superior memorabilia and spare parts, including, in very limited quantities, complete SS100 motorcycles again.

The Brough Superior SS100 tribute replica shown here, on display at Garage Classics Museum, Williamstown, Australia, features Lawrence of Arabia artwork on the fuel tank. The replica bike sports a 1200 Shovel Head H-D motor, and an Attitude rigid frame. The builder is Leigh Goodall.

Robert Creemers, New Zealand

Already a classic racing competitor on a '62 Manx 500 and a '37 Norton Manx 500, Robert wanted something more for vintage-class events. When Ken McIntosh from McIntosh Racing told him that the Brough Superior was the quickest bike in its day for this class, and didn't know of any racing nowadays, they decided to look around for one, and eventually found the bike shown here in the UK in 2005. The bike went to auction (in poor condition), and Robert purchased and brought it to New Zealand. After an engine blow-up, Ken worked his magic on it and, along with a brand new frame, barrels and other parts invested in it, the bike is now immaculate and performs beautifully on the race track.

The airbrush painting of Lawrence of Arabia was done in 2011 by www.airbrushasylum.com.au.

Robert Creemer's racing Brough with NZ fern tree forest backdrop.

The glorious JAP-made SS100 engine has a bore and stroke of 86mm x 99mm respectively, and capacity is 1150cc. The bike features high level 1⅞in diameter pipes, with cast aluminium finned manifolds (as made by Brough) and barrel-type mufflers.

SPECIFICATIONS
1927 Brough-Superior SS100 made by George Brough in Nottingham, UK

Owner: Robert Creemers, Auckland
Restored by: McIntosh Racing, Auckland
Engine type and displacement: 50-degree V-twin Engine made by JA Prestwich Ltd, Tottenham, London, UK (JAP). Rebuilt by McIntosh Racing using cylinders and heads made in 1929 by UK firm Hemmings Engineering
Transmission: 'Sturmey-Archer' brand three-speed 'hit and miss' foot change
Forks: Brough-made 'Castle' forks based on a 1925 type Harley-Davidson leading-link design, but modified to take large friction type shock absorbers and steering damper
Chassis: Brough-designed full cradle frame with triple chain stays, giving much greater rigidity then contemporary frames and setting new standards of handling
Dimensions: Wheelbase 1450mm. Weight 175kg
Suspension: Front – 'Castle' leading-link forks. Rear – none
Gas tank: The nickel-plated 16-litre 'torpedo' tank, designed by George Brough in 1922, with racing type twin filler caps is one of the signature features of a Brough-Superior
Mudguards: Racing-type steel mudguards
Seat: 'Lycette' brand mattress type fully sprung saddle
Wheels: 'Enfield' brand wheels – 21in front wheel with 7in drum brake, 19in rear wheel with 8in drum brake and rubber block type cush-drive for the rear sprocket

Ken: "The Brough-Superior was advertised prior to WW2 as 'The Rolls-Royce of Motorcycles,' and the SS100 was the most expensive model offered; a position it still holds in the vintage motorcycle market.

"This bike has been largely re-constructed in New Zealand by McIntosh Racing with major help from Steve Raffills and Neville Bull.

"It has been ridden by the owner, Rob Creemers at 110mph at Pukekohe, where it has won numerous Vintage Class races, easily exceeding the makers claim of having exceed 100mph when sold new.

"The bike is incredibly stable at all speeds, leading to the maker's claim of 'Hands off at 100mph,' but still corners with perfect precision at all speeds."

BSA

BSA (Birmingham Small Arms Company Limited) was founded 1861 in Small Heath, Birmingham, and was a major industrial group, manufacturing, amongst others things: firearms, bicycles, motorcycles, cars and buses. Motor bicycles were added to bicycle products in 1910, and, in 1919, BSA launched its first 770cc V-twin. During the Second World War, the army chose the 500cc side-valve BSA M20 motorcycle as its preferred machine for war duties. Post-war demand led to the Small Heath factory turning entirely to motorcycle production. Other British brands were amalgamated over time, and the purchase of Triumph Motorcycles in 1951 led to BSA becoming the largest producer of motorcycles in the world at that time.

By 1965, however, competition from Japan and Europe was cutting into BSA's market share. Poor investments in new products in the motorcycle division and the subsequent loss of sales led to problems for the group, and, by 1968, the end was near. In 1971, reorganisation resulted in BSA motorcycle production moving to Triumph's Meriden site.

A rescue operation, organized by the British government in 1972, led to the takeover of remaining operations by Manganese Bronze Holdings, the then owner of Norton-Villiers, resulting in Norton-Villiers-Triumph. Although the BSA name was left out of the new group's name, a few products continued to carry it until 1973.

Scott Colosimo's 1954 600cc BSA M21 Custom

Scott always fancied a modern take on a British classic, so when a worn out BSA M21 came up for sale on eBay, his project was on.

BSA produced the M21 until 1963. The model, which was also used by the British Army in World War II, was the last side-valve built in Britain.

The bike was stripped, and given a much needed frame and engine overhaul. Next, the exhaust received some attention. New wheels and front fork (Suzuki GSX R1000) were chosen for a beefier look than the stock bike. The front discs/rotors are GSX-R600 items and the rears are GSX-R750.

Scott is the founder of Cleveland Cycle Werks, so some items for his personal ride were sourced in-house.

Scott: "This bike was built to be ridden, it's not polished, it has dings, it's been dumped and ridden hard."

A nice modern take on a British classic.

The BSA is CCW's Scott Colosimo's personal ride.

Two XS650 19in front wheels were fitted; one heavily modified to serve as a rear.

Cretingham Crank Company, Cretingham, UK
Culyer B31 BSA

This bike was created by Gilbert Sills, ex-race mechanic and genius-in-metal.

The frame is a modified B31 swingarm, replaced by rigid rear single cycle-type seat mounting. The fuel tank is a modified Francis Barnet item with integral oil tank.

SPECIFICATIONS
Engine: BSA B31 350cc single 1947
Gearbox: Standard four-speed BSA
Forks: Standard BSA B31
Front hub: Standard B31
Rear hub: Standard B31
Wheels: Standard B31 powder-coated and pin-striped
Clutch: Home-made belt drive unit and cover
Exhaust: Custom-made with re-packable aluminium silencers
Photos by Andy Culyer, owner

Lävi Avikainen, Home Grown Choppers, Finland

Lävi's beautiful Hermans Racing-labelled custom BSA single was the first prize winner in the Classic Custom section of the Norrtälje Custom Bike Show 2011. This annual event is a hub for Swedish and Scandinavian custom bike builders, see www.custombikeshow.se

The aluminium oil tank was made by Isto Kotavuopio, and depicts Urho Kekkonen's head (the former president of Finland).

The paint of the bike is mixed with three different colours. The bike sports competition components, like the rear axle mount (drag racing), the rear chassis design (speedway), clutch and front rim (speedway). The carburettor is a rare 1950s Amal GP1.

Others involved in this BSA project, which has also engaged in racing, were Tarmo Kotavuopio, Tomppa Turunen, Jude Packalén, Robin Backman, Juha Halonen, Flake Torppala, Lipsi Lintunen, Ryhti-Iki, and Amoila Kromaamo.

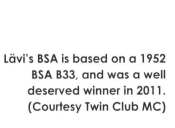

Lävi's BSA is based on a 1952 BSA B33, and was a well deserved winner in 2011. (Courtesy Twin Club MC)

Lamb Precision Engineering, UK
Son of a Gun

This has been one of the most successful UK bikes ever built. Son of a Gun won the AMD Alexandra Palace 2011 event (British Championship), and the European Championship in Mainz, Germany (the first UK bike to do this). On top of this, the bike was awarded second place in the AMD World Championship 2011, Sturgis USA. The next page showcases a variety of BSA hardtail customs.

This BSA single-based custom had 1400-plus hours spent on it, and it shows! The exhaust is by Expressive Motorcycles, and the leatherwork is by Scott. (Courtesy Nick Crocker)

This bike was photographed at the VBMC 2009 Euro Bike Rally, Prince William County Fairground, formerly in Leesburg. (Courtesy Don Broxson)

Spotted at the 'Donut Derelicts' Saturday morning meet in Huntington Beach, California. (Courtesy Ray Nessel)

Parked at the West London Harley Riders Burning Budgie Rally 2011. (Courtesy Ray Douglas)

The Spark in the Dark BSA A10, built and owned by Sooty, was photographed at the Barrel Bikers Custom Show, Milton Keynes, UK, August 2012. (Courtesy Trevor Earl)

This bike, named Hardly Dangerous, was photographed at the Gilmore Car Museum Antique Motorcycle Show in Hickory Corners, Michigan. (Courtesy Pete Walsh)

The front end features a BSA M20 girder, modified to fit onto the 1965 frame. (Courtesy Scott Pease)

The GasBox, United States

The GasBox was opened in 2009 by Jesse Bassett, and specialises in custom fabrication and vintage motorcycles. Jesse has over thirteen years of mechanical and fabrication experience, including engine rebuilding, repairing, restoring, customising, and building motorcycles.

Jesse began the 1965 BSA project in 2009, when a customer brought in a rigid chopper to be customised. Jesse completely stripped the bike, and retained only the engine, frame, and stock BSA QD rear wheel.

Jesse's customer, Brett Scully, wanted to have a girder fork, and so, after some time, one was sourced from a BSA M20. Jesse had to fabricate a new top clamp, neck stem, and new linkage, and used antique faucet handles for the friction ride control because of the look of the porcelain and brass. By adjusting the rake, offset, and height of the fork, he was able to obtain the correct frame stance.

The rear wheel is a stock BSA item, 18in powder-coated black with stainless spokes and Coker tyre. The front wheel is a thirty-six spoke 21in item, laced to a BSA Bantam hub and fitted with an Avon tyre.

The fuel tank began as a oil-in-frame Triumph item that has been chopped and fitted with late model Harley-style rubber mounts. Jesse found a local die maker to duplicate the BSA golden flash emblems

SPECIFICATIONS

Engine: BSA 650cc Lightning, polished and completely rebuilt
Frame: Custom hardtail stock BSA
Front end: BSA M20 girder, modified to fit onto a 1965 frame
Front wheel: 21in modified BSA bantam hub
Rear wheel: 18in BSA QD hub modified BSA drum
Mudguard: Modified Wassell
Fuel tank: Modified Triumph OIF
Oil tank: Hand-made, fitted with BSA cap and fittings
Carb: Amal 389 monobloc
Ignition: Boyer
Tail light: 1930s Dodge
Headlight: 1930s MG
Exhaust: Hand-made stainless steel
Handlebars: Hand-made
Levers: Cook replica of pre-war British style
Seat: Jason's Custom Upholstery
Paint: Black with gold leaf by Jerry's House of Kolor
Polish and nickel plate: Jason's Show Quality Metal Finishing
All fabrication and assembly was done by Jesse Bassett at The GasBox in Cleveland, Ohio

and cast them in brass for the tank. Jesse fabricated the oil tank from scratch, then fitted the cap and fittings of a 1960s BSA stock item, and rubber mounted it to the frame.

The entire engine was disassembled and polished. The sludge traps were cleaned, the notorious BSA crank bushing was upgraded, and the cylinders were fitted with the next size over 9:1 compression pistons. Jesse fabricated the exhaust from stainless steel, and styled it after the BSA high scrambler pipes. All of the electrical items were upgraded to Boyer.

The handlebars were made to act as part of the top clamp for the girder. The levers are Cook replicas of pre-war British bikes. The grips are made of the same leather as the seat. The headlight (not shown) is a mudguard light from an early MG (modified to adapt to the girder).

The paint is black with gold-leaf and red striping by Jerry Koenigsmark of Jerry's House of Kolor. The leather work was done by Jason's Custom Upholstery. All of the polishing and nickel plating was done by Jason's Show Quality Metal Finishing.

LC Fabrications, Virginia, United States

Jeremy Cupp founded LC Fabrications in an effort to keep his passion for motorcycles, machines, and anything with wheels alive.

LC Fabrications specialises in custom parts for Sportsters and modern Triumphs, but if asked, will put nearly anything into metal, as the following BSA custom below demonstrates.

Birmingham Beeliner

Shane Ramey: "This project was originally planned to be a simple rigid wet frame daily rider. I approached Jeremy of LC Fabrications for his

The Beeliner was part of the AMD 2009 World Championship-Freestyle Class, and the Smoke Out 10 winner.

help on building a hardtail section of the frame, but we soon decided to make it a full-on build. The red Warp 9 wheels and tyres were from a Honda dirt bike that I had dual-sported. My friend, Dan Doughton, donated the '73 Triumph OIF, which was the backbone of this project.

"We wanted to keep the bottom of the frame three inches off the ground, but still run a 21in front wheel, so the backbone was lengthened three inches and relieved a few degrees, along with two inches added to the up-stretch.

"The hardtail was also made in-house, along with the paint and seat. Jeremy designed the girder front end that we made, which works well with the Fox Vanilla R shock. Since the bike was so narrow we discarded the idea of running a conventional gas tank. We turned the wet frame oil tank into the gas tank. It holds about 1.5 gallons, and the gas gets to the Mikuni carb by the way of a vacuum fuel pump from a lawnmower.

"The rear axle is fixed, so we made up a chain tensioner with heim joints. I always wanted a jockey shift so we moved the shifter to the left side, and modified the stock controls to accept a clutch pedal. Much of the bike was built out of junk lying around the shop. A five inch exhaust elbow was used for the oil tank. The headlights were from Jeremy's old race mountain bike, and a few old British exhaust sets donated their bends to help the motor exhale. The rear brake was removed from a 250R Honda. The engine used is a '67 BSA A65T that was purchased from a yard sale.

"The cases were split and freshened up to stock specs except for a 0.020in overbore. Carburation is a Mikuni 32mm with a Clay Cobb sidedraught intake manifold. The Joe Hunt magneto was purchased through eBay along with the Peterbilt shift knob. The steering stabiliser from an old cold water knob that was on my Grandma's basement steps was used.

"Jeremy and I have become good friends during this build, and now I am an involved member of LC Fabrications."

HESKETH

Hesketh Motorcycles was founded in 1980 by Alexander, the third Lord Hesketh, and based in Daventry and Easton Neston. The first prototype, using a special Weslake engine, was running in the spring of 1980. It wasn't until 1982, that a purpose-built factory was set up to manufacture the Hesketh brand in Daventry. Sadly, the bike in its various guises wasn't a success in the marketplace, due in part to under-development, and the company closed again in 1984.

Broom Development Engineering, based at Turweston Aerodrome, continued servicing the marque's clients as well as offering modifications to make the bike reliable. It also produced a small production run per annum, but a downturn in the motorcycle market and lack of funds hampered further progress. In 2010, the Hesketh Motorcycle business was taken over by Paul Sleeman, who now operates the brand out of Surrey, and has his sights firmly set on bringing the marque to its next level.

The Hesketh was primarily a gentleman's tourer, but one model, named the Vortan, although a sports version, warrants a place here. Only one Vortan was ever produced.

The Hesketh Owners Club 30th anniversary magazine reported: "In 1988 Mick Broom shocked the world at the UK Design Expo with the Vortan. A styling exercise in collaboration with a young designer Lionel Dean produced a 'street fighter' that was five years ahead of the Ducati Monster (1993) and Triumph Speed Triple (1994). The aim was to show that the Hesketh business was very much alive, and to provide a vehicle for development of a range of new ideas, such as the 1100cc engine and a novel hydraulically-sprung and damped rear suspension. It's a pity funding was not immediately forthcoming to develop this further as it was way ahead of its time. The mock-up has since become an item of lasting curiosity." (Courtesy HOC)

**A Hesketh on display at the Birmingham Barber Museum.
(Courtesy Rogério Machado)**

The Vortan's engine capacity was increased to 1100cc with a longer stroke, steel crank, different ignition, cams and cylinder heads. (Courtesy David Sharp)

The 992cc (60.5in³) Hesketh in British Racing Green. (Courtesy Chuck Nissley)

The Vortan's chassis was completely new, with lighter components to give better performance and steering.

CHAPTER 2
Indian (UK)- Panther

INDIAN (UK)

Although the Dakota 4 motor is not a British engine, it deserves to be part of the book, since the machine was created by an Englishman and was produced in Scotland (with Swedish technology). Alan Forbes trademarked the Indian brand in the early '90s as his own, and set about reviving the 4. He has been in the Indian Motorcycle restoration and parts supply business for thirty years.

Alan: "Indian in the UK is not Polaris and have no connection to them. There have been several concerns that have come and gone claiming the Indian name in other territories during the time the UK company has been producing Indians. Indian UK has been producing new Indians over many decades and are registered trademark holders for the Indian Motorcycle in the UK. Some bikes are also sold under the Dakota trademark."

The 112.6in³/1845cc Indian Classic De Luxe.

SPECIFICATIONS
Frame: Cradle, triple braced. Seamless tubular steel
Rake: 31 degrees
Rear suspension: Spring shock absorber. Adjustable air optional
Front fork: Telescopic
Front brake: Dual 12.6in disc. Hydraulically activated
Rear brake: Internal expanding
Final drive: Cardan shaft
Rear tyre: 170/80/15
Front tyre: 130/90/16
Overall length: 98.82in
Overall width: 19.69in
Overall height: 47.05in
Wheelbase: 68.5in
Ground clearance: 4.5in (3.94in with air shock absorbers)
Weight: 750lb (full tanks)
Fuel capacity: Five gallons
Range: 200 miles
Fuel consumption: 40 miles per gallon @ 60mph
Motor: Inline four-cylinder, four-stroke
Cooling: Air
Displacement: 112.6in³/1845cc
Valve system: OHV, 2 per cylinder
Bore & stroke: 3.374 x 3.15 / 85.7mm x 80mm
Compression ratio: 7.5:1
Maximum rpm: 4400
Fuel supply: Multi-port sequential fuel-injection
Ignition: Electronic ignition
Starting: Electric
Power: 95bhp @ 3800rpm
Torque: 150lb/ft @ 3809rpm

The Dakota-badged Classic De Luxe.

JAP

JA Prestwich Industries was founded by John Alfred Prestwich in Tottenham in 1895, and its engine division came to be known as JAP.

After 1945, production was taken over by Villiers Ltd, and the company was completely absorbed by the Villiers Engineering Co in

1957, just as Villiers itself was to be taken over by Manganese Bronze Bearings.

JAP engines were sold to many famous motorcycle marques, such as Brough Superior, Triumph, AJS, and HRD, as well as to French and German motorcycle manufacturers.

JAP engines were associated with racing success, and were still used in speedway bikes well into the 1960s.

Fast forward to today, and JAP V-twin engines are still being made in the UK by the Card brothers, the sons of the late Alec Card, and the current proprietors of the marque's name.

Anssi Kantonen's JAP, Jyväskylä, Finland

Anssi built this fine supercharged JAP, which some motoring publications decided to name a 'Rough Superior.' His idea was to make a slightly customed Brough Superior-style racer. Anssi manufactured the frame and the fuel/oil tank himself. The front end is modified from an early British Zenith. The Supercharger is AMR with SU HS4 carburettor. Very nice, indeed.

The bike sports a 1938 JAP MT 750cc V-twin (bored to 810cc), and the front fork is a Zenith Girder 'Druid' item.

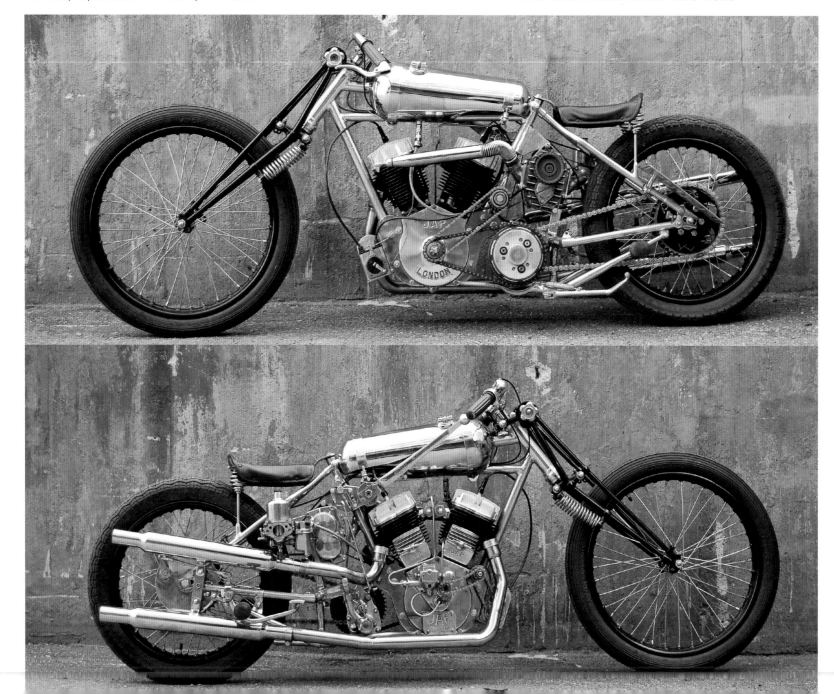

SPECIFICATIONS

Exhaust type: British made, unknown
Transmission: Sturmey Archer/Hurth/Grasstrack clutch
Chassis type: Steel frame, British racing style
Dimensions: Length total: 2180mm. Wheelbase: 1530mm. Seat height: 670mm
Suspension type: Sprig (front)
Fuel tank type: Steel fuel/oil
Mudguards: None
Seat: Dunlop, England
Wheels: Rear 18in Bridgestone, front 21in Avon Speedmaster
Special features: AMR supercharger, SU HS4 carburettor

Larry Houghton, Lamb Precision Engineering, UK
Spirit of Endeavour JAP custom

Larry Houghton conceived the idea of a hardtail-framed, JAP-engined custom bike in early 2010, when talking to the Card brothers at the Alexandra Palace Custom Show in London. The Cards are the proprietors of the JAP marque's name, and exhibited their late father's 1320cc JAP V-twin motorcycle on their trade stand at the same event.

As a result of this meeting, Larry acquired a number of sets of crankcases and further parts to assemble half a dozen engines. Two years of R&D later, Larry and his mate Maff from Expressive Motorcycles, with whom Larry shares the same premises, redesigned/rebuilt the initial platform in such a way that the only original engine components were the crankcases, barrels and cylinder heads. As an example of the pair's redesign, amongst many other modifications, the cylinder heads can now be removed in less than half an hour.

A single downtube front frame, with the 1320cc engine as a stressed member, had a one-off, bolt-on hardtail unit fitted to it for the desired vintage look.

A Super E carburettor was mounted to a one-off inlet manifold, with a specially-machined aluminium velocity stack. The two-into-two exhaust system was fabricated from 2in diameter stainless tube. A RevTech five-speed kicker gearbox was added for practical reasons. A pair of H-D-style springer forks from Zero Engineering was fitted without any need for modifications, while the wheels are 17in Excel rims, laced to anodised Talon hubs, and shod with Michelin racing wets. The petrol tank originated from a New Hudson from the 1930s. The seat was stitched by Scott Lloyd Motorcycle seats in Bournemouth, while the initially blank rear mudguard came from Ray Fisher's Britbits Emporium. The cream and black paintwork was done by Joeby's Airbrush Art in Wells, the powder-coating by Nick from Reality Motorworks, Bristol. Polishing was Hi-Pol, Gosport's job, and, finally, plating was done by Dorsetware Ltd in Poole.

The main objective of the build was to use as many British components as possible, and to act as a showcase for British talent.

The intention from the outset was/is to build six bikes a year in either bobber or cafe racer style, while using Metisse frames. Prices will be around £37,000 for the totally hand-built machines. Lamb Engineering has no association or agreement with JAP Industries.

One-off single downtube front loop with engine as a stressed member, one-off bolt-on hardtail, H-D style Zero Engineering springer forks. (Courtesy Mike Prior)

Restored 1930s New Hudson single filler petrol tank, oval Biltwell oil tank from Zodiac.

The 1320cc JAP OHV V-twin, redesigned/rebuilt by Lamb Engineering & Expressive Motorcycles. This is definitely one of England's finest bikes.

SPECIFICATIONS
Gearbox: Norton Doll's Head
Frame: Ariel
Front forks: 1932 Matchless
Front hub: Triumph
Rear hub: Triumph
Wheels: Borrani aluminium, 19in
Silencers: Custom-made 'Brooklands' copy

"The engine in this bike, I believe, came from a forklift truck, working in a carpet factory in Kidderminster. It is a 750cc side-valve 50-degree V-twin, made in 1927 by JA Prestwich of Tottenham, London.

"A few mods were done to it: a major reworking of the porting, a larger inlet manifold, and the compression ratio raised from 4.2 to 5.

"The total loss lubrication system was reworked, with a small tank under the gearbox which the engine vents into, and then a small pump mounted atop the tank being manually operated then pumps the oil back into the main oil tank.

"The frame is a 1947 Ariel with 1932 Matchless girder forks fitted to it.

"The gearbox is a 1930s Norton Doll's Head type. The clutch is still Norton with an in-house-made belt primary drive and cover.

"The exhaust and silencers were all made in-house. The fuel tank, oil tank and fillers were also made in-house.

"Being an ex-race mechanic, I couldn't resist making a racer out of it, and I also have a keen interest in '30s bike styling, so I strived to build a '30s style Brooklands racer.

"For an engine that is 85 years old it goes very well. It accelerates quicker than the 1323cc DTZ."

MATCHLESS

Matchless was founded in 1899 by Henry Collier & Sons. The marque's output ranged from small capacity two-strokes to 750cc four-stroke twins. Matchless and AJS were amalgamated into Associated Motorcycles (AMC) in 1938, whereby both companies continued producing models under their own names. The '60s marked the time when the Matchless four-stroke twin was replaced with the Norton twin*. Matchless production ceased in 1966.

Matchless also supplied V-twin engines to power Morgan's three-wheelers from 1933 to 1935. Morgan's Super Sports model was built from 1927-1939. The company also supplied engines to Brough Superior from 1935 to 1940.

*Associated Motor Cycles (AMC) was founded in 1938, as a parent company for the Matchless and AJS brands. AMC later absorbed James, Francis-Barnett, and Norton.

A 1934 Morgan Super Sports. (Courtesy Adrian Pingstone)

A Matchless chopper 650 1961, at the NEC Birmingham Classic Car and Bike Show 2012. (Courtesy Bob Lovelock)

Javier Lombardo, Argentina

Javier's bike is a 1949 Matchless G3L, 350cc, four-speed. He brought it back to life with the following modifications: The exhaust is hand-made, the front fork, front and rear rims are from a Kawasaki Vulcan 500. The fuel tank, engine and gearbox are original items.

(Left & above): Before and after restoration.
(Courtesy Javier Lombardo)

This bike was photographed at the British Iron Association of Massachusetts spring show 2011. (Courtesy Steve McKelvie)

NORTON

Norton was founded in 1898 by James Lansdowne Norton in Birmingham. Manufacturing began in 1902, initially with bought-in engines, but from 1908 a Norton-built engine appeared, thus beginning a long line of fine motorcycles and racing success.

In 1953, the business contracted, and Associated Motor Cycles bought Norton shares. Sales picked up again during the '50s due to high demand for the Dominator and Atlas twins, especially in the United States.

1968 marked the arrival of the 750cc Commando model, with the engine/gearbox/swingarm insulated from the frame by a series of

A true-blue British hybrid bobber. (Courtesy Nick Crocker)

freedom

Freedom is when nothing inhibits your desire to move in the best possible way. Equate that to bikes and it becomes a vital factor. Norton have always taken the freedom movement seriously, the Commando 750 Hi-rider is fine proof of that. This new version of the Commando Superbike is styled exclusively for the rider who requires the distinctive appeal of a chopper but without its inherent handling defects. Vibration, the prison of many a good machine, was eliminated on the Hi-rider (and on all Commandos) by the revolutionary Isolastic construction – the turbine smooth ride has to be unfelt to be believed. Power, so often unuseable unless aided by constant gearchanging,is big, dynamic and flexible, leaving you free to appreciate the ride. Roadholding, backed by years of Norton competition success is unsurpassed, ensuring a greater degree of mobility. Acceleration, the Hi-rider can outgun almost anything off the freeway. Commando comfort, second to none, guarantees freedom from fatigue. Maintenance, reduced to a minimum by the uncomplicated big twin formula. If the Hi-rider is not your style, freedom of choice within the Commando range offers the right combination to suit every individual. On all counts the Norton Commando allows the rider unfettered opportunity to get the very best from both himself and the bike. Why accept anything less?

Norton
Commando 750's
-all with the isolastic super-ride

The Commando Hi-Rider. (Andover-Norton)

rubber mountings. The resulting absence of vibration found favour with the public, and the Norton Commando became a best-seller. The bike was voted 'Motorcycle of the Year' several years running in the UK.

The BSA-Triumph group faced difficulties at the time, and proposed a merger with Norton, but although Norton Motorcycles was by far the smaller partner, Norton's management effectively secured a take-over of BSA-Triumph, leading to the formation of Norton-Villiers-Triumph (NVT). Sadly, subsequent political manoeuvring led to NVT's demise.

In 2008, Stuart Garner bought the rights to Norton, and the Norton name resurfaced in the UK with a modern restyle of the Norton Commando of old, and plans for the development of the NRV588 racer.

Norton's Hi-Rider model was an attempt at a contender for the US 'soft chopper' market; something Japanese manufacturers pursued with their midrange soft chopper models right into the 1980s.

It was a case of how to convert a sports motorcycle into a chopper for American tastes. The bike was kitted out with ape hanger handlebars, a nine-litre fuel tank, a new seat with an integrated sissybar, and a small headlamp.

The model was not considered for European markets, and only about 50 were sold in the US. Despite this, the bike remained in Norton's lineup for several years.

The Norton shown above was apparently first created by Pete Gordon in Hove, UK. The bottom end stems from a Norton Atlas, while the cylinder head came from a Commando model.

The frame originates from a 1955 Ariel. Quomp Customs in Hampshire overhauled the rear plungers and the engine. A Boyer Bransden Power Box and Lucas K2F magneto eliminate the need for a battery. The fuel tank is a 1960s Harley Sportster item. Owner Lorne added the sprung solo seat, mudguard, and oil tank.

William Cochran, Denver, Colorado

William gives the rundown on his chopper: "The front hoop on the frame is from a late '50s, early '60s BSA. The rear section is all custom. I hand-drafted the axle plates too, but heavier, but they still work with the original Norton drum brake setup. I built the oil tank from a piece of 5in exhaust tube to give it its old-style look. The rear mudguard was a mid '30s Ford spare tyre cover that I managed to find in a junk yard. While grinding and sanding that mudguard, I learned a valuable lesson: wear a respirator, or at least a mask, when working with old parts. Breathing that old lead paint had me down for a day or two. I built the mudguard struts from some ½in round stock. I used a 32 Ford light to make the tail light. The front end is kind of a hybrid of Norton and Harley items."

William and his mount.

This unique Norton chopper is a blast from the past. The late Mick Fish from Wigan, UK built this custom bike. It's fitted with two front wheels.

The twin front fork custom. Mick won the best engineering prize at the Kent Custom Show in 1986 for his chopper. (Courtesy Nick Crocker)

The motor is a 1975 850 Commando engine. It has a Sonny Angel manifold mated to a Clay Cobb Sidewinder intake. On the end of that is a Mikuni VM42 Carb.

Norton single chopper

Nick Crocker took the pictures of this customized Norton single at a gathering in the UK. Nick: "I can't tell too much about the bike, apart from that it is hand-painted (brush), and the handlebar grips are made from Spitfire cannon shell cases ... All I know about its owner/builder is he is based somewhere in Wiltshire, and he did all the work himself – a true garage-built bike!

A very nice vintage chop. The original platform for this custom seems to be Norton's ES2, a model first produced in 1927.

Jeff Monteith's Norton, Canada

Jeff, who hails from Fredericton, NB tells the story: "I bought, in 2002, a good running, non numbers-matching '69 Norton Commando 750 Roadster from Gary Cooper of Olde English Motorcycles in Saint John, NB. That winter Jeff cut the frame and disassembled the bike to initiate the future build of a clean, lean, Norton café bobber. A lot of dust collected on the project, and six years later, Jeff passed the project in boxes to Rick Waite, a talented and self taught mechanic and fabricator, open to new ideas, using old school techniques and quality.

Rick finished Jeff's bike that winter – the frame was extended out 8in to a hardtail, still using the original downtube and front frame, to keep the Isolastic rubber engine mounts. The ignition was changed to a 12v Boyer with a battery eliminator kit to increase spark at start. A Hurst jockey shift was installed, and pivots where the tachometer cable used to come out." (For more info: www.capitalcitytoystore.ca)

Thanks to Mark Appleton (www.britcycle.com), for putting me in touch with Jeff.

What a machine! The wrapped dual fishtail exhaust produces a healthy soundtrack.

SPECIFICATIONS

Wheelbase: 64.5in
Seat height: 22.5in
Overall length: 89.75in
Engine: Stock 1969 745cc Norton twin
Transmission: Stock four-speed transmission
Wheels: Stock front wheel with Avon Speedmaster tyre, 16in Harley drop centre wheel with Avon Mk2 rear tyre
Carburettor: Stock 32mm Amal carburettors

Stock Norton Roadhandler forks feature external helper springs, and the stock Roadster gas tank was sanded to bare metal before being clear-coated.

Larry Houghton, Lamb Precision Engineering, UK

Larry Houghton, British custom bike builder extraordinaire, started this stunning custom bike project in 2008 with a very neglected 1976 850cc Norton Commando, sourced from a friend. The engine and gearbox, cylinder heads and barrels got sent for bead blasting and powder-coating in red, after which he rebuilt the motor. The engine's new radical forward inclination required modifying one of the internal arterial oilways to eliminate the risk of oil starvation.

Larry then fabricated one-off aluminium velocity stacks and inlet manifolds, joined by dual 932 Amal Concentric carburettors.

Maf Welch from Expressive Motorcycles created the one-off, 2in bore two-into-two exhaust pipes. He also did all the wiring for the bike.

The standard four-speed gearbox was converted to right-hand operation by Larry, while the power to the gearbox is transferred by a triplex Norton primary chain.

The one-off aluminium primary drive cover was also Larry's handiwork.

The frame and swingarm consist of six individually-machined sections.

The spine section runs down the back of the engine and functions as an anchor point for fuel and oil tank. The central section has the gearbox and engine mounts attached, and also provides points for the shock absorber, coils, footrest mounts and swinging arm spindle. The one-off, twin-spar type swingarm is held by three big bolts, and also holds the shock's rear mount nicely.

The steering head has a fully adjustable headstock, enabling the front end's trail and rake to be adjusted according to personal preference. The CNC machined fuel tank (hewn from a solid block of acrylic) can also pivot, which changes the angle of the solo seat (made from ¾in acrylic sheet) to complement any adjustments that may have been made to the frame's geometry.

The front single downtube section curves to fit in front of the engine's barrels. It also has a pivot to allow the adjustment of the steering head angle.

The lower downtube is actually a separate bolt-on piece.

Upside down forks of the Suzuki K5 type were sourced from eBay and placed into one-off yokes, whereby the top yoke doubles as an instrument housing and holds the handlebars.

The custom mudguards were made from clear acrylic sheet, and are retained by one-off aluminium mounts.

Five-spoke Harrison floating discs and a pair of Harrison Billet 4 calipers take care of the braking department.

The 21in front and 23in rear wheels are, again, one-offs, machined by Larry from blanks, showing radiused rims and three curved and tapered spokes (sourced from V2 Customs in the States).

The rear wheel bearings, brake disc and drive sprocket are mounted outboard of the swing arm's twin spars.

Powder-coating was taken care of by Wessex Metal Finishers in Salisbury, while Hi-Pol in Gosport did the polishing job, and LW Customs in Salisbury did the paintwork.

What more is there to say, other than that Larry has flown the British flag quite high again with Cafe Rouge. It is even more intriguing that the whole build only cost him about £4000 (not counting four months' labour of love)!

Awards: 11th place AMD World Championships, Sturgis, USA, 2008. 10th place European Championships. Best in show Bulldog Bash UK. *Back Street Heroes* Bike of the Year 2008. Best in show, Pecquencourt. Best freestyle, Rosmalen Netherlands.

The Norton engine is slanted at 40 degrees, with the gearbox piggy-backed behind the motor.

BRITISH CUSTOM MOTORCYCLES

The Café Rouge in all its transparent glory. The CNC machined fuel tank can pivot, changing the angle of the solo seat, and is a custom one-off. The bike features two-inch bore, two-into-two exhaust pipes. (Courtesy Horst Roesler)

PANTHER

Phelon and Moore was founded in 1904 in Cleckheaton, Yorkshire, and produced motorcycles under the Panther name. The design, first launched in 1924, involved a large, 40-degree inclined, single-cylinder engine, patented in 1900 by Joah Phelon & Harry Rayner. This model spanned the entire history of the company, in configurations ranging from 500cc to 645cc versions. Panthers were often used for hauling sidecars. Production ceased in 1966.

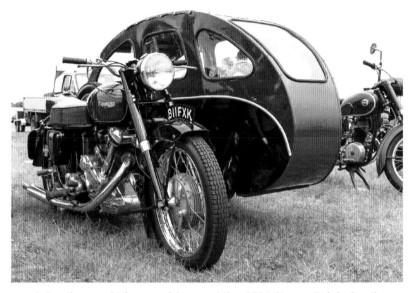

A Panther and Viceroy sidecar at the 2011 Steam Fair in South Cerney, Gloucestershire, UK. (Courtesy Andrew Farmer)

On display at a classic/custom bike show at The Royal Bath and West Showground, UK. (Courtesy Peter Wort)

This Panther was customized by Ifan Owens. The bike is fitted with electronic ignition, the wheels are from an old Honda FT; it has Suzuki GSX disc brakes, Honda FT forks, and a Citroën 2CV alternator. A lot of work went into fitting all these modifications.
(Courtesy John Tokarz)

The angle of the engine flows nicely with the rigid rear frame of this Panther custom. (Courtesy David Brentley)

Ben Graham's Panther
Panthemonium Panther M100/M120

Ben: "The engine and frame of this bike were married up in 2007, by Gilbert Sills of the Cretingham Crank Company. Gilbert bought a job lot of Panther parts, together with a fairly original Panther 120 some years previously. He ran the Panther for several years and sold it in 2007. I'd always coveted it and missed the boat when it was sold, so I asked if he happened to have another one. Indeed he did – but it was in bits. Unbelievably, the engine had sat idle under the previous owner's bench in the same position for over 35 years – as proven by a corrosion hollow caused by constantly dripping rain – and the frame was bare and rusting. There was no tank, but pretty much everything else was rusting in old wooden crates. We discussed a few ideas, much influenced by Gilbert's desire to lighten the weighty brute, which is driven by his motor-racing heritage. Most ideas were completely mad, and we settled on what you see – a fairly extraordinary rendition of a Panther. Much of it is stock, but the details are what make it stand out – the beautiful Brough-inspired tank, the rigid 120 back end, the stainless bars and big Royal Enfield headlight, and the utterly amazing pipes, silencers and seat arrangement. The bike's fun to ride and handles really well. However, the best thing about this bike is that wherever you park it, people stop and stare, and jaws do literally drop!"

SPECIFICATIONS
Builder: Cretingham Crank Company, Cretingham, UK
Transmission: Four-speed Burman
Fuel tank: Cretingham Crank Company
Paintwork: Ben Graham
Forks: Panther 120, telescopic
Chassis: Modified Panther 120, 1961. Rigid
Dimensions: Wheelbase 60in
Suspension: Rigid rear
Mudguards: From the scraps bin
Seat: Custom-made by Cretingham Crank Company. This sits on a Ford Transit leaf-spring and acts as very effective suspension
Wheels: Panther M120, 19in
Prizes/awards/placements: Fenman Classic Specials Class, Runner-Up 2007

The bike started life as a 1938 Panther 100, 598cc 'sloper,' OHV, 87mm x 100mm. The custom pipes are by Competition Fabrications, and the repackable silencers are by the Cretingham Crank Company.

CHAPTER 3
Royal Enfield-Sunbeam

ROYAL ENFIELD

The Enfield Cycle Company, based in Redditch, Worcestershire, had its brand name Royal Enfield licensed by the Crown in 1890. In 1909, Royal Enfield introduced a small motorcycle with a 2¼hp V-twin Motosacoche engine. In 1912, the JAP 6hp, 770cc V-twin with sidecar combination came on the market, and made Enfield a household name. In 1913, the factory produced its own 425cc V-twin, which, in 350cc guise, almost won the 1914 junior TT at the Isle of Man. In 1930, the model K, 976cc side-valve V-twin power plant was introduced (updated in 1937 with its displacement increased to 1140cc). The cylinders then featured detachable iron heads and enclosed valve gear, with a redesigned crankcase. Other model designations like Bullet, Crusader, Meteor, Super Meteor, Constellation or Interceptor are synonymous with the brand.

The company was sold in 1968 to Norton-Villiers-Triumph (NVT) and production ceased in 1970. The company slogan 'Made like a gun, runs like a bullet,' (a nod to its weapons manufacturing division), stuck with the firm throughout its history.

In 1956, Enfield of India started building 350cc Bullet motorcycles from UK components under licence, and, by 1962, was producing complete bikes. In 1995, Enfield of India bought the rights to use the Royal Enfield name.

Manufacturing of Royal Enfield motorcycles in Chennai is alive and well, and the marque is now the oldest motorcycle brand in the world still in production, with the Bullet model enjoying the longest motorcycle production run of all time. Royal Enfield's new 500cc unit construction motor, combined with a rumour that, by 2015, the company plans to release a parallel twin with a nod to the Meteor twin of old, sees the marque's future shining bright.

Who knows, one day the factory in Chennai might also consider reviving the V-twin configuration.

Ted Klatt's Royal Enfield, Winnipeg, Manitoba, Canada

Ted: "Being a hot-rodder at heart (for over 40 years), I built a lot of the parts for this RE custom and wired the bike in my garage on a

Can't wait to see a new Royal Enfield big twin.

The engine is from a 1968 Royal Enfield Interceptor.

SPECIFICATIONS

Engine: Stock 750cc 180-degree twin
Transmission: Stock four-speed, one-up three-down, stock neutral finder, right side shift
Frame: Stock stretched a lot, rear hardtailed, stock rake
Front suspension: Stock Enfield, Norton Roadhandler
Rear tyres: Rear 16 x 5
Fuel tank: Modified Triumph I had lying around
Mudguard: Stock front. Full length on rear, stock stays
Seat: Sprung Bates style
Pipes: Home-made, crossed legs, wrapped
Handlebars: Repo Clubman
Gauges: Aftermarket Mini speedo and tach
Headlight: Came with the bike
Controls: Stock, Anderson pegs
Brakes: Stock Enfield drums, dual leading-front

budget over a three-year period, using basic hand tools, keeping the bloodlines Enfield.

"Parts fabricated by myself are: Gas tank and cap; 'Oil' tank and cap, used to store tools since it's a wet sump motor; tail light, hammered out of a piece of exhaust pipe, polished; DoT truck lens; 75 six-sided pointy nuts hand filed in a vise and polished over 150 hours; exhaust is just

The exhaust system is home-made, and the frame carries the Royal Enfield logo.

The front wheel is stock 1999 Royal Enfield 3.25 x 19.

This is the author's former ride: a 350cc Royal Enfield. He had it shipped to New Zealand in 2004 following a holiday in India. Frequent conversations about the bike at traffic lights vouched for its appeal with the public. The bike was fitted with an Indian-made 20-litre fuel tank, front drum brake from a 500cc model, and an aftermarket exhaust.

exhaust pipe from parts store wrapped in heat wrap formed for crossed legs; hardtailed and stretched rear frame using ERW tubing, backbone and downtube are stock; velocity stacks made from expandable flex pipe; battery box; coil bracket; kick-stand; mini hub cover on front wheel; assorted brackets throughout; entire wiring system; side-mount license plate; all the welding and bodywork; paint (black), prepped myself, sprayed by master painter friend Rick Ponsac."

Royal Enfield's 2009 model harks back to the G2 Bullet of the early '50s, and retains the British style that is inextricably linked to the world's oldest motorcycle manufacturer.

The heart of the matter is the 500cc unit construction engine (UCE), with electronic fuel injection. It replaced the four-speed, iron-barrelled engine that had been in continuous production for over 50 years.

The Bullet Classic's highly polished engine cases, 18in wheels, and two-tone paint scheme exude an authentic charm. The Classic comes with a solo seat as standard, with dual seat and pillion seat pad options available.

A new Royal Enfield Bullet Classic on display December 1st 2008 at the International Motor Cycle Show NEC, Birmingham, UK. (Courtesy Dennis Goodwin)

A number of individuals have used Royal Enfield's new engine as a platform for customising.

Rick Fairless – Strokers Dallas, Texas, United States

Rick Fairless, custom bike builder and owner of Strokers Dallas built this RE custom from the ground up to join his personal stable of bikes.

His mission with this project was to make this bike the COOLEST ROYAL ENFIELD ON THE PLANET! Did he accomplish his mission, what do you think? The bike, named Myrna, was unveiled in December 2011 at the International Motorcycle Show (IMS) at Dallas Convention Center (DCC).

Myrna started life as a 2011 Royal Enfield C5 Bullet. (Courtesy Gene Slater)

Many items on this bike, like the frame and exhaust, were designed in-house.

SPECIFICATIONS

Design and fabrication: Rick Fairless/Strokers Dallas
Displacement: 500cc
Transmission: Five-speed
Air cleaner: Rick Fairless/Strokers Dallas
Exhaust: Rick Fairless/Strokers Dallas
Paint: Other Side Customs
Frame: Rick Fairless/Strokers Dallas
Handlebar controls: Rick Fairless/Strokers Dallas
Rear mudguards: Rick Fairless/Strokers Dallas
Tail light/brake light: Rick Fairless/Strokers Dallas
Pegs: Rick Fairless/Strokers Dallas
Foot controls: Rick Fairless/Strokers Dallas
Dual fuel tank: Rick Fairless/Strokers Dallas
Oil tank: Rick Fairless/Strokers Dallas
Seat: Rick Fairless/Strokers Dallas
Grips: Rick Fairless/Strokers Dallas
Wheels: 140/70/21in front and rear
Tyres: Marathon
Brakes: Performance machine
Fuel tank cap: Crime Scene Inc
Shocks: Fournale
Swingarm: Modified by Rick Fairless/Strokers Dallas
Kickstart: Rick Fairless/Strokers Dallas
Intake manifold: Rick Fairless/Strokers Dallas
Mudguard: Rick Fairless/Strokers Dallas
Brake drive system: Rick Fairless/Strokers Dallas

This custom RE was created by *Sideburn* magazine. Photographed at the Motorcycle Live 2011 show in the UK.
(Courtesy Royal Enfield UK)

Magrette Enfield, New Zealand

In 2011, Magrette Timepieces watchmaker Dion McAsey commissioned Ross from New Zealand's Bat out of Hell Customz n Classics in Whakatane to build him an old-school racer out of an equally old Royal Enfield 500cc single.

Ross set about creating a design which, though it could be classed as minimal, is bold enough to make a statement.

Wheels and hubs came from an earlier Bullet model, while the originally Triumph-based frame had its steering head section altered to fit the larger 1in bore required for the Bat out of Hell springer fork and triple clamps. The brake hubs' internals were machined, and more efficient units fitted inside to improve on the original anchors.

The old 1920s racer look-alike turned out pretty cool, so owner Dion decided to produce a 2012 timepiece, based on the Magrette Bullet. (Photos courtesy of Kevin Kinghan).

The Royal Bobber by Chopper Squad, Worcestershire, UK.
Photographed at the Motorcycle Live 2011 show in the UK.
(Courtesy Royal Enfield UK)

The old cast iron 500cc engine was reconditioned and polished, and many custom fabricated items fitted. Neat touches abound, like the billet aluminium velocity stack breathing through a stainless steel tea strainer!
The back section was rebuilt to become a rigid rear.

Old Empire Motorcycles, UK

Alec Sharp: "Old Empire Motorcycles was born through an absolute and enduring passion for everything two-wheeled. Previous experience gained through working at a similar enterprise only further fuelled a desire to put our own stamp and style on the motorcycle world and show people what we really can do.

"'Pure Motorcycle' sums up how we like to design and create our

motorcycles, taking a back-to-basics, stripped down approach to produce rideable motorcycles in their purest form.

"The Pup emphasizes our 'Pure Motorcycle' motto, and holds it close to its thumping heart. It takes you back to the fundamentals of motorcycling, where handlebars, a seat, some wheels, and an engine is all that is needed to enjoy the 'purity' of riding a British-built, hand-made custom motorcycle. A blend of bobber and boardtracker, the Pup is a perfect mixture of old and new.

"Its namesake is the Sopwith Pup, a World War One biplane flown by the RAF in its infancy; its small size and manoeuvrability made it a popular choice for young British pilots, which, we felt, was apt, as our Pup seems to share those very same characteristics. It is the resulting product of using modern day engineering and reliability in a combination with the sleek and classic aesthetics of a bygone era."

The Pup features an Amal 900 concentric carburettor conversion kit.

SPECIFICATIONS

Donor bike: 2008-2009 Royal Enfield Electra
Wheels: 19in, with Avon roadrunners
Frame: Custom-made, fixed axle with chain tensioner
Number plate: Custom-made, bracket and Lucas rear light
Fuel tank: Custom-made, scalloped, with leather knee pads
Forks: Modified Aprilia RS50 yokes, fork legs re-chromed, shaved, and lowered 1.5in
Front brake: Modified Aprilia RS50 caliper with Royal Enfield disc. Remote Grimeca front brake master cylinder
Rear brake: Royal Enfield drum
Foot controls: Modified
Saddle: Brooks sprung leather saddle and grips (modified)
Instruments: Koso electronic speedo with warning lights
Indicators: Front and rear chrome oval LED stalk indicators
Headlight: Mini Bates
Handlebars: Stainless steel custom
Controls: Replica chrome choke, decompression lever, indicator switch and high/low beam switch. Chrome Doherty levers
Cables: All custom-made
Sidestand: Custom-made
Headstock: Custom-made, taper roller bearing cups
Electrics: Cloth-covered PVC wiring, brass ties. Nano-gel battery, new relays, ignition switch and toggle switches
Exhaust: Custom stainless steel with mini baffle
Mudguards: Aluminium
Paint: Fuel tank, guards and headlight with pinstriping
Frame: Powder-coated frame and attachments
Brightwork: Chromed/painted/polished/scotched engine, gearbox and attachments

Hitchcocks Motorcycles, UK

Hitchcocks in the UK offers many parts and kits for customising Royal Enfields. Opposite we see a nice rigid conversion of a Bullet model.

SPECIFICATIONS

Engine: 500cc Royal Enfield Bullet
Exhaust: Early 1950s style
Transmission: Standard four-speed
Forks: Standard forks with period top yoke
Chassis: Standard frame converted to rigid with bolt-on kit
Dimensions: 53.5in wheelbase, 153kg approx dry weight
Suspension: Standard
Fuel tank: Standard
Mudguards: Standard front, period rear
Seat: Period single seat from the 1950s
Wheels: Standard

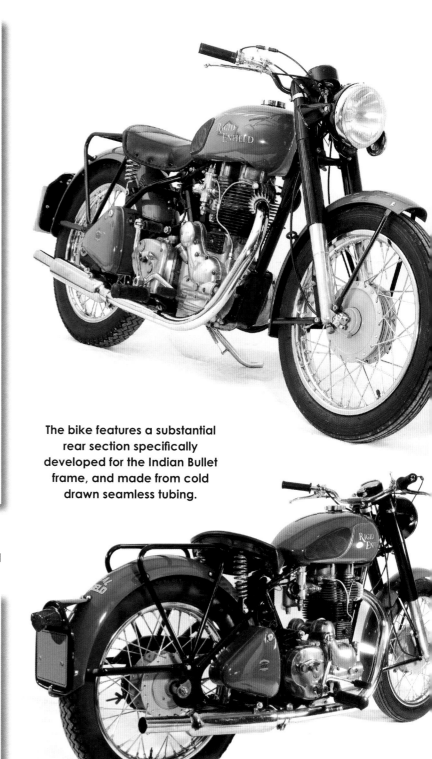

The bike features a substantial rear section specifically developed for the Indian Bullet frame, and made from cold drawn seamless tubing.

Next up is an Enfield custom built by Dave Barker from Speedmetal Cycles in Denver, Colorado. His build was inspired by old board track bikes. He claims this bike topped out at 101mph according to his friend's speedo.

The two examples of old Royal Enfield V-twins below, are themselves followed by contemporary V-twin offerings. It remains to be seen if the factory in India decides to adopt such designs (in this case from Carberry in Australia and Aniket Vardhan in the United States), at some stage in the future.

Dave fabricated the tank, headset cover, rear fender, 4in longer swingarm, struts and hand shift lever. The aluminium wheels are custom-made 21in front and rear. (Courtesy Cory Grunkemeyer)

Vintage Royal Enfield V-twin spotted in 2006 by Steve Jones.

Jari Vuorela's 1930 Royal Enfield 1140cc V-twin – 'The world's fastest Royal Enfield.' On display at the 2012 Helsinki Motorbike Show. (Courtesy Dave Smith)

Aniket's Musket 700cc on one of its first outings.

Aniket Vardhan, United States

Aniket, an Indian industrial design teacher based in Columbus, Ohio, excited Royal Enfield enthusiasts with his original 'Musket' 700cc V-twin motorcycle in using two cast iron 350cc cylinder heads to create this, let's call it stage 1, V-twin powered bike.

The one-off Royal Enfield Musket 700cc looked very appealing, and sounded as good as it looked; a V-twin beat emanating from its classic-looking, air-cooled 700cc engine.

Now enter stage 2. Aniket decided to take his V-twin to the next level by coming up with a 998cc version of his initial concept. The upgraded 998cc V-twin engine now uses two 499cc cast iron cylinders. The pre-unit construction is retained as it is, with the engine block, gearbox and clutch housed independently.

The V-twin engine uses the standard Royal Enfield cylinder heads, the cylinders, and the pistons. The four-speed gearbox, replete with the neutral finder, has a right-shifting gear lever, with the brake to the left, in line with the retro design of this engine. The 998cc V-twin motor is placed in a Royal Enfield motorcycle with a modified frame. In time, however, a brand new frame will probably be made to house this custom-made engine.

Aniket intends putting the Royal Enfield 998 Musket engine into serial production, hence the motor is designed with small-scale production in mind.

The Musket's engine has been beautifully crafted, and the bike conveys a nice vintage look. The 59-degree, 998cc V-twin motor keeps the retro look true to tradition with external oil lines.

Carberry Enfield, Australia

The concept of this Royal Enfield V-twin was conceived by Paul Carberry and brought to fruition by Paul and Ian Drysdale (builder of the Drysdale 750-V8 and 1000-V8), and is already for sale in Australia.

The basic premise was to create a classic-style 1000cc British V-twin, sourcing as many standard Royal Enfield parts as possible. The aim was to create a cruiser with the torque, look, feel and sound of traditional British bikes, but with enough technology to make it a practical everyday proposition.

A 55-degree V configuration was chosen for a combination of style, balance and mechanical simplicity. The design allowed the hydraulic lifters to be accommodated above the standard Royal Enfield cams without modification to the barrels. The standard Enfield primary drive cover was also retained. The Enfield clutch was strengthened, and a larger engine sprocket fitted to utilise the extra performance of the V-twin.

The Carberry engine with lean burn cylinder heads. (Courtesy Luka Carberry)

This Café Racer-style Carberry Royal Enfield looks like it means business. (Courtesy Luke Ray, _Fuel Magazine_)

A Carberry Enfield on display at the 2011 Australian Moto GP at Phillip Island. (Courtesy Murray Wilson)

SUNBEAM

Sunbeam was founded in 1888 by John Marston, and produced bicycles and motorcycles in Wolverhampton from 1912 to 1956. The Sunbeam trademark was sold to and operated by Associated Motor Cycles Ltd (AMC) from 1937-1943, whereupon BSA took over ownership of the name. BSA produced Sunbeam motorcycles in Redditch, Worcestershire from 1946 to 1956.

The shaft-drive Sunbeam S7 first saw the light in 1946, powered by a 500cc twin-cylinder engine, mounted longitudinally in a fully sprung frame. The S7 Deluxe and S8 variants followed later. The S8 was marketed as a sports version, with the frame having a more conventional seating arrangement, rather than the S7's cantilevered seat. Other differences included a sportier aluminium silencer and slimmer tyres than the S7's balloon tyres.

A rare Sunbeam trike photographed at the annual SOF rally in Ashbourne in England's Peak District. The bike's owner is Clive Martin. (Courtesy Hans J Knitsch)

A Sunbeam S7 fitted with a custom seat photographed at the Sandbach service station in 2009, just south of Manchester on the M6 motorway.
(Courtesy Robin Drysdale)

Destiny Cycles, UK

Vic Jefford always fancied an S7 Sunbeam; a bike classed as a gentleman's tourer in the '40s and '50s.

An S8 model, however, although in bits, turned up at an autojumble. After a clean up and reassembly, the engine started on the third kick. The clutch and gearbox both worked and were left untouched.

Vic decided that the S8 deserved more than just a standard rebuild. He powder-coated the tank and mudguards satin black, and the wheels were done in red, with Melissa Gee doing the pinstriping by hand. The seat is a Mid West Choppers' item, the handlebars came from Derek, and the new yokes were made by Woody. The re-laced wheels were fitted with a set of W&W tyres, which came from Richard Millard. The rest of the bike remained standard Sunbeam S8.

The original exhaust was no longer usable, and hence replaced with a one-off Destiny Cycles item. A new kickstart, ammeter and a replica headlight were sourced from Sunbeam expert Stewart Engineering in Leamington Spa.

It took Vic just one month to do the entire rebuild.

A Sunbeam S8 with ape hanger handlebars. The colour combination works well.

Roger Müller's bobber, Switzerland

Roger's custom is based on the Sunbeam S7.

SPECIFICATIONS
Handlebar/hidden throttle: Home-made
Battery box: From the original Sunbeam S7, but adapted alongside the frame (also incorporates the horn)
Fuel tank: From a Victoria bike
Other: The seat fasteners and fuel lines are from copper and brass, the mudguard brackets, tank mounting, light and horn switch bracket on the handlebar are home-made

(And opposite): The bike is fitted with 5.00-16 Firestone Champion de luxe black tyres.
The 1951 500cc parallel-twin produces 26hp, and the tail light and saddle bag come from a Condor A580 Swiss army bike.
(Courtesy Romeo Hutter)

CHAPTER 4
Triumph

Triumph Engineering Co Ltd was founded by German expatriate Siegfried Bettmann in 1885 in Coventry, initially producing bicycles and importing sewing machines from Germany. From 1898 onwards, Triumph extended its production to also include motorcycles, initially from its unit in Nuremberg, Germany, but later also in Coventry.

During World War I, Triumph supplied more than 30,000 motorcycles to the Allies. By the mid 1920s, the company had become one of Britain's main motorcycle and car manufacturers, and, by 1929, Triumph sold its German subsidiary of the business. In 1936, the company's car and motorcycle divisions became separate companies. The motorcycle operation was acquired by Jack Sangster, and began exporting Triumphs to the United States (quickly becoming a key market for the company). Sangster employed Edward Turner, who then penned the 500cc Triumph Speed Twin, released in 1937, thus providing the template for all Triumph twins until the 1980s.

An X75 at Brielow Bar in the High Peak, Derbyshire, UK 2011. (Courtesy Andrew Johnston)

The Craig Vetter-designed Triumph X75 fame spread far and wide. This one is on display in a museum in Akureyri, Iceland. (Courtesy Magnús Sveinsson)

Motorcycle production at Coventry was affected by the Coventry Blitz in World War II, and production restarted at Meriden in the West Midlands in 1942.

In 1950, Edward Turner built a 650cc version of the Triumph Speed Twin, named the Thunderbird. One year after the Thunderbird's release, a race version of the bike, with a twin-carb head, hot cams and high compression pistons, reached 132mph at Utah's Bonneville Salt Flats.

Triumph motorcycles also received considerable exposure in the United States through the movie *The Wild One*, featuring Marlon Brando riding a 1950s Triumph Thunderbird.

In 1959, the first Triumph to bear the famous Bonneville name was the T120, a tuned double-carburettor version of the Tiger T110 model.

From 1963 on, all Triumph engines were of unit construction.

By 1969, despite Triumph holding 50 per cent of the US market for motorcycles over 500cc, the company struggled to keep up with the technical advances of Japanese offerings, marking the beginning of the end for the company.

Triumph Motorcycles was resurrected by John Bloor in the 1980s, and, by 1987, the company had completed its first engine. The following year, Bloor funded the setup of a new factory in Hinckley, Leicestershire. Production of new models built up slowly but steadily from 1992, and by 2000 Triumph was breaking even and has been going strong ever since.

Triumph produced its X-75 Hurricane model from 1972-1973, a factory special credited with inventing the cruiser category. The bike was designed by Craig Vetter in the United States.

The Triumph TSX was a lowrider-styled Triumph for the North American market, the first TSX being produced in June 1981.

Essentially a re-styled Bonneville, the TSX featured a lowered chassis and 16in rear wheel, along with such modifications as a stepped seat, shortened mudguards and exhausts, and Morris alloy wheels. Production lasted until 1983.

A US-based Triumph TSX, restored by Stuart Rust.
(Courtesy Giannis Ragias)

Hardtail Bonnie with coffin tank, photographed at the 2009 VBMC Euro Bike Rally, Prince William County Fairground. (Courtesy Don Broxson)

A Bonnie in bobber style photographed at the 2009 VBMC Euro Bike Rally, Prince William County Fairground. (Courtesy Don Broxson)

Another Cretingham Crank Company build. Engine: 770cc Triumph unit-construction bottom end with eight-valve Weslake top end, Nourish pushrods and cams. Mudguards: Custom-made in carbon fibre. (Courtesy Andy Culyer)

There's something special about a twin-engined custom bike, as the attention bestowed on this Triumph double-engined salt racer indicates. The racer has a 1350cc capacity. (Courtesy Chris Cullen)

Triumph twin-based customs have popped up alongside custom Harleys since the advent of the chopper/bobber scene, although Harleys always dominated this segment of motorcycling.

One fine example of firms having built lots of pre-1970 Triumph customs is ACME Choppers, Meredith, NH, United States. This family business, established in 2005, offers everything from forks and frames to rollers and ground up custom builds. ACME has the tools, talent and experience to do your projects proud, as the examples shown here amply illustrate.

Top right: ACME Choppers' blue and white Triumph with ape hangers.

Above: ACME Choppers' white and black bobber-style custom.

Right: The frame of ACME Choppers' Green Flake Triumph has a 1967 front mated to a David Bird loop hardtail. (Courtesy ACME)

ACME Choppers' Raw Metal Triumph, built in five days in 2010 for a biker build-off at Laconia bike week.

SPECIFICATIONS
Engine: 1968 motor with a 750 big bore kit and a Joe Hunt magneto.
Carburettor: Fabricated stainless steel, 90-degree sidedraught intake to fit the Mikuni carburettor, also the adapter was made to fit the Dennis Goodson air cleaner.
Forks: ACME wide springer front forks and fabricated oddball drop wishbone front legs to give it a '60s style.
Handlebars: Stainless '60s-style T-bars, made to match the looks and lines of the front end.
Wheels: 21 x 2.15 Invader wheel in the front, with a Speedmaster tyre, and a 16x3 Invader on the back (from a Sportster). Axle and spacers made to fit.
Seat: Jay at Truckalope Leather.
Mudguard and sissy bars: Fabricated and chromed.
Oil tank: 5.000 round alloy unit, made and polished by ACME. Old Harley oil filter hidden down between the rails of the hardtail.

This 1971 Triumph T100 Bobber by ACME Choppers went to auction on eBay.

SPECIFICATIONS:
Frame: 1968 Triumph with a one-off hardtail.
Engine: 1970 Triumph T120R; the head modified with a threaded insert to fit the V-band clamps to hold the exhaust.
Exhaust: Slip fit stainless two-into-one, finished with a shortened Supertrapp.
Front end: Sportster item, shortened by 3in and the mounts shaved off.
Handlebars: Aluminium ACME trees and a vintage Aris headlight mounted. Also sports 2in aluminium ACME risers and stainless Hot Rod Bars, along with ACME BMX grips, off the shelf and bolted on. Brembo master cylinder installed.
Fuel tank: Villain tank, narrowed and shortened, and topped with Mooneyes fuel cap.
Mudguards: 7Metal West aluminium ribbed mudguard, ⅛in thick, rear mudguard topped with an After Hours Choppers tail light.
Wheels: 18in rear and 19in front, fitted with vintage style Firestone tyres.

ACME Choppers' Hinckley Triumph build.

SPECIFICATIONS
Frame: ACME custom frame
Forks: ACME Wide Glide trees with turned-down fork sliders
Handlebars: ACME risers with custom handlebars
Fabrication: All custom fabrication work done in-house
Wheels: Road King Wheels with Firestone tyres
Engine: Modern Triumph Bonneville engine
Other: ACME billet grips. Trick oil cooler deflector guard

SPECIFICATIONS
Engine: Triumph Bonneville 865cc (bore/stroke) 90 x 68mm
Carburettor: Keihin
Exhaust: Gietl-Bikes
Transmission: Five-speed (original)
Secondary drive: Chain
Power: 75hp @ 7500rpm
Torque: 72nm @ 5800rpm
Maximum speed: 180km/h
Fork: CCE Springer, 2in under stock
Brakes: Front DNA four-piston; rear DNA four-piston brake pinion
Mudguard: Front Gietl Bikes; rear Penz/Gietl-Bikes
Footrests: Gietl-Bikes
Tank: CCE modified
Oil tank (fake): Gietl Bikes (for electrics)
Spotlight: Bates style P & W
Tail light: Kellerman three-in-one
Dry weight: 220kg
Wheelbase: 1680mm

ACME: "We built this custom Hinckley chopper frame based on our proven ACME Loop tail chopper construction and geometry. The finished product has a badass stance, great ground clearance, a nice tight steer tube angle and perfect proportions."

A recent trend involves the use of late model, Hinckley-built Triumph engines in customising projects.

GIETL-BIKES GmbH, Wernberg-Koeblitz, Germany

Raimund Gietl's shop has gone down the Hinckley Triumph chop route. Here are two examples.

Christian: "The Brown Sugar was built in the winter of 2011-2012.

The front wheel is a DNA Big Spoke, 2.15 x 21in with MH90 21 Metzeler whitewalls. The rear tyre is an 8.5 x 18 Metzeler 240/40-18 whitewall. Chassis is a Penz/Gietl Bikes rigid frame. (Courtesy Horst Roesler)

My dad built himself a Hinckley Bonnie hotrod bobber the winter before, and his bobber, with the Triumph engine and springer fork, struck a chord with me, in that I wanted to build a Hinckley chop myself."

Brown Sugar won the 22-year-old tool mechanic trainee (who helps his dad after work) the German *Custombike* magazine competition in 2012.

Christian's aim was to build a bike that would look completely different to all the other motorcycles that had left the workshop.

A crash-damaged 2005 T100 was the source for the engine, oil cooler, ECU, and carburettor. The engine was painted gloss black, the exhaust and air filter replaced with tuning parts, and a Penz rigid frame, meant for a 240 rear tyre, was acquired.

Christian fabricated the handlebar (with an integrated Motogadget speedo), the seat bracket (with integrated mountain bike shock absorbers), and the removable front mudguard. The footrests, extending the tank to hide the ignition lock, and the fake oil tank (which housed the electricals), followed on.

Christian also did the Marrakech-Brown and light ivory paint-job, as well as the pinstripes. The competition win is quite a testament to the skills of this first-time bike builder.

The Lollipop-Chop features a Zodiac Mustang fuel tank with psychedelic paint job. The rear wheel runs on 5.5 x 18 with a 180/55-18 Metzeler. (Courtesy Christian Gietl)

The Lollipop-chop was built for a customer who wanted a '70s-style look, but which used modern technology (so he could spend more time riding the bike rather than working on it).

SPECIFICATIONS

Engine: Triumph Speedmaster 865cc, (bore/stroke) 90 x 68mm
Fuel injection system: Keihin
Exhaust: Gietl-Bikes
Transmission: Five-speed (original)
Secondary drive: Chain
Power: 65hp @ 7500rpm
Torque: 74nm @ 5800rpm
Maximum speed: 180km/h
Frame: Zodiac/Gietl Bikes rigid frame
Front wheel: 60-spoke wheel chrome 2, 15 x 21 with MH90 21 Metzeler
Brakes: Front, DNA four-piston; rear, original Triumph two-piston
Handlebar: Gietl Bikes tiny speedometer with integrated Motogadget.
Mudguard: Front: Gietl Bikes rear: Penz
Footrests: Gietl-Bikes
Oil tank (fake): Gietl-Bikes (for electrics)
Spotlight: Bates style P & W
Tail light: Kellerman three-in-one
Dry weight: 210kg
Wheelbase: 1780mm

LC Fabrications, Virginia, United States
TT De Luxe

Jeremy: "This bike started when I saw one of the scramblers on eBay. I then told a friend of mine, running a salvage business to be on the look out for a new Triumph. Soon after he found a black '06 Bonneville on an auction that had smoke damage. We wound up winning it for $300.00!

"As winter drew I decided to use this for a donor bike – something a little different from the norm, while being modern and reliable, and yet still cool. So I had a power plant, and no idea what to build around it. I did some research on 1900s to 1930s European bikes of all types, and tried to make a mental note of what was cool. I suppose that the main things that stuck out were the tank style (loosely after a 1910 Triumph), the druid style front end, the knobbies, centre stand, and friction steering dampener.

"For the frame, I went with a lugged design for some extra detail, and made the cradle removable to help stick with that European style.

"Early one Saturday morning, I loosely sketched the café boat tail thing, and wow – it looked awesome. I went to the shop the next morning and got started bending up some rod! I suppose this is where the whole project shifted gears from classy antique custom to 1900-ish café racer sort of thing. Race bike in mind, the two-into-one Lakester pipes and drop bars fit naturally. The inverted levers are sourced from Dave Cook and are the very first set of stainless levers he has ever made.

LC Fabrications' Druid-style front end.

The two-into-one exhaust was made by LC Fabrications, and the carburettors are Keihin CRs. TT Deluxe was sixth in the AMD 2009 World Championship Freestyle, the Smoke Out 9 winner, and Easyriders National VQ Award winner.

SPECIFICATIONS

Fabrication: LC Fabrications
Year and make: 2008 Special Construction
Model: TT Deluxe
Assembly by: LC Fabrications
Time: Six months
Chroming: None
Engine year: 2006
Rebuilder: Jeremy Cupp
Ignition: Nology
Displacement: 865cc
Air cleaner: Strom 97
Transmission: Jackshafted final drive
Painting and moulding: LC Fabrications
Painter: LC Fabrications
Colour: Black/Tan
Paint type: Chromabase
Frame builder: LC Fabrications
Rake: 28in or so
Other frame details: Removable cradle
Handlebars: LC Fabrications
Headlight: eBay
Tail light: LC Fabrications
Front pegs: LC Fabrications
Electrics: LC Fabrications
Fuel tank: LC Fabrications
Seat: Jeremy and Lindsay Cupp
Forks: Druid/LC Fabrications. Friction dampers
Wheels: Front, 19in, conical mini drum hub; rear, 19in hub, H-D rim
Tyres: Firestone military bias
Brakes: Drum on jackshaft

The front end is from a 2003 gixer, and the trees were made in-house. LC Fab didn't need the dual disc front, so cut off one side, as well as the fender mounts, which allowed for the 1in drop and 2in larger diameter front tyre.

"For paint, I wanted to stay sort of scalloped style. The logos on the tank are copper leaf versions of the 1910-1914 Triumph logo. My wife, Lindsay, and I spent evenings at the kitchen table doing the leather-work. The wiring on this bike was probably the biggest challenge. I sat down with a factory diagram, the original harness, and a volt-ohm meter; around 30 or so hours later I had myself what is apparently the first ever chopper-style wiring schematic for a modern Triumph."

Bonnie

Jeremy: "This project, just called Bonnie, really started out as a good deal on a Maryland Salvage bike I bought with the sole intention of fixing for resale. She'd been hit in the rear and dropped, but a little tweaking of the swing arm, a new rear mudguard and seat, and a coat of paint did her justice.

"I rode this bike all year long, procrastinating on listing it for sale. This Triumph is light and agile, quick, cool, and most importantly

dependable. As much as I loved it, however, I decided to do a little cutting and see what came out of it. It was hard at first to chop up a reliable new bike, but once the swing arm and rear section were gone, so was the reluctance. I made a weld-on tail section for the stock frame. It is made of .120 DOM and has 1in of drop and 2in of stretch. I re-used as many of the stock parts as I could, which allowed for ease of assembly and a low-cost project.

"The wheels both use the stock hubs, which I powder-coated black, and laced them to Sun rims using Buchanan spokes, and wrapped them with Avon rubber. The brakes are stock rotors and calipers, although I had to pull a few tricks out of the bag to make it all fit. The rear master

**Jeremy really likes the style of So-Cal British bike, and thought a Hinckley Triumph version would be nice.
The frame is a 2007 Triumph/LC Fabrications type: stock with welded-on hardtail.**

cylinder linkage was inspired by Fab Kevin's X-15, and I used the bowl of an old Amal carb for the fluid reservoir. The pegs and foot controls are all stock, while the hand controls are from an R1 Yamaha.

"The stock pipes, as well as two sets of old British pipes and a Harley muffler, all gave of themselves to create the two-into-one exhaust. The seat is one of those twenty-dollar Bates rip-offs, which I reshaped and did my own leather. The lighting was all pulled from my stock of random swap meet finds, and the rear mudguard was fashioned from an old Chevy spare tyre cover.

"I reused the stock tank as well, mostly because I wasn't looking for a full-on custom bike, just a cool little version of a Bonneville. I cut the pinchwelds off, dished the sides a bit more, and added a rib and a badge to the top to mimic the mounting hole plug on the older Brits. Paint, again, was kept very simple and done in the style of a 1949

SPECIFICATIONS

Owner: Jeremy Cupp
Fabrication: LC Fabrications
Year: 2007
Model: Bonneville T100
Assembly: LC Fabrications
Time: Three months
Engine: Air-cooled parallel twin
Ignition: Nology
Displacement: 865cc
Air cleaner: Emgo
Pipes: LC Fab two-into-one
Handlebars: ⅞in dirtbike (cheap)
Risers: '71 Bonneville
Mudguards: Front, none; rear, Chevy spare tyre cover
Headlight: 5¾in swap meet (cheap)
Tail light: Swap meet
Speedo: Wind in the face
Pegs: Stock Triumph
Hand controls: Yamaha R1
Wiring: LC Fabrications
Fuel tank: Modified stock
Seat: LC Fabrications
Forks: inverted hydraulic Showa (from 2001 GSXR)
Wheels: Front, 21in, stock Triumph hub, Buchanan Sun rim, Buchanan SS spokes; rear, 18in, Triumph hub, Buchanan Sun rim, Buchanan SS spokes, Avon tyres
Brakes: Stock Triumph
Powder-coating: Spraylat Gloss Black by Shickel Corp
Paint: DuPont Chrysler silver
Painter: LC Fabrications
Lettering: LC Fabrications

The forks are Harley-Davidson, and the rigid frame was sourced from Cycle-One.

Triumph. Adam at Shickel Corp in Bridgewater VA did the powder on the frame."

Michael Williams, East TN, United States

Mike: "I bought the bike as a wreck from an insurance sale, it started life as a 2007 Triumph Speedmaster. The front wheel is 80-spoke, the twisted rear wheel is stock Triumph for 2006. There is no front mudguard, the rear mudguard is an aftermarket item, redone to fit the bike. The seat is flamed leather by La Rosa. I fabricated lots of sheet metal, and also wired the bike and custom-fabbed the exhaust. The controls are all stock Triumph. The paint job was done by Roy's Body Works and DRCUSTOMS. It has a base of silver mini flake paint with pearl. I generally do not name my bikes, but this one needs to be called 'Hardass' because of the difficulty I had to build it. It runs great and gets lots of attention."

Shawn Zammit, Australia

Shawn: "I bought a Triumph Bonneville T100 brand new in 2005 with the sole intention of chopping it up. The resulting custom was built to be a modern interpretation of '30s/'50s' bobbers. It had to be lightweight, slim, short, and fun to ride. I'm not into 'rat' bikes, so I finished it the best

I could with the budget and talent I had. Having said that, though, it's not a show bike either. It gets ridden to work most days, plus on weekends with friends.

"I called her Winona, because she's a rider. (Winona Ryder).

"I built the bike myself in my parents' garage, which took me 4½ years to do. There are only two things I didn't do; namely, the paint job and the wiring harness. The bike was built in Wollongong but I'm based in Sydney.

"It's an air-cooled parallel twin 865cc engine left standard, including the carbs and transmission. The engine was repainted to suit.

"The bike has standard headers with shortened standard mufflers and custom end caps. (Left muffler on right side and right muffler on left to get the up-swept look).

"I kept the original front end, but shaved the glides (lower legs), shaved top and triple trees, modified 1978 T140 risers with drag bars.

"The original frame is smoothed, with shaved gussets and a lengthened swingarm that has been strutted to look like a hardtail.

"The bike is one inch lower, three inches longer in the wheelbase, and is now 180kg wet.

The seat is from a 2010 Triumph Daytona 675, and rides on 3in springs. The bike has been converted to belt-drive, the front wheel is a 21in alloy Akront rim laced to a 1972 Honda CB750 front hub, and Triumph T100 tank badges serve as footpegs.

"The fuel tank is from a Suzuki VS750 with a custom petrol cap.

"The rear mudguard is a Honda VTX 1800 front mudguard. Mudguard rails were made to suit. The front mudguard is alloy.

"Rear wheel is an 18in alloy Akront rim laced to a '72 CB750 front hub. Standard Triumph brake calipers with Honda CB750 discs.

"Honda VT750 headlight. Stop light was a salt and pepper shaker, and has a Land Rover red lens.

"Lastly, the bike has a custom alloy front pulley and Buell XB12 rear pulley."

Jens Endrulat

Eisenherz Kraftrad, Germany

Jens built his custom, named Tin Lizzy, based on a 2007 Triumph America platform. The bike was favourably received at the Tridays gathering in Austria and the German Custombike Championship in 2009.

Patrick Coulomb, France

Patrick comes from Nice in France. He disassembled his Triumph Thruxton for its engine, ordered a custom frame from the USA (after a long search), and then set about exchanging parts and fitting attachments for the frame (manufactured by aluminium welder David).

Patrick: "The construction took almost a year for the whole motorcycle, with Lionel doing the wiring harness and me all the rest of it. I am very happy to say that the bobber works perfectly."

SPECIFICATIONS
Manufacturers: Patrick, David (aluminium), Lionel (electrics)
Owner: Patrick
Engine: Thruxton 2004, Dinojet 3 kit, K&N air filter
Exhaust: Stainless steel custom
Fork: Sportster
Suspension: None
Hugger: Aluminium
Saddle: Aluminium with spring pin
Footrests: Aluminium
Box for electrics: Aluminium
Wheels: Front 21in, rear 16in

The aluminium fuel tank holds nine litres, and the frame stems from Cycle One Manufacturing USA. (Courtesy Alban Montalbano)

Officine GP Design, Italy
Triumph Bonneville Essentia

Luca & Fabio Pozzato's stunning Triumph Bonneville creation was commissioned by its female owner, Stefania, and required more than just some welding, as the pictures show. The custom, named Essentia ('essence' in Greek, and meaning 'what it was to be') took six months to build, and used a variety of materials, such as steel, wood, aluminium alloy, bronze and leather.

The Bonneville Essentia is part of GP Design workshop's ONLY FOR YOU programme.

The bike sports Brembo floating disc brakes, Kineo rims, H-D springer fork, Rizoma aftermarket parts, an RK chain, a brown suede leather saddle, Monza model fuel cap, and an old-style tail light. The rear mudguard is made from sheet metal, and was covered with rosewood by a master cabinet maker. The paint job is glossy and multi-layered to give a tortoise-shell effect. The intake manifold is made of

steel, the manufacturing technique being the same as used for the manufacture of the exhaust manifolds.

Triumph's big twin Thunderbird model is starting to get the custom treatment, too. Here are two examples:

Rock'n'Ride Bikerstore, Munich, Germany
Dennis Hopper Tribute Thunderbird

The Munich-based Triumph Rock 'n Ride store has dedicated this Thunderbird to the deceased actor.

Harald Schmiedt: "There are men, real men, and there are legends. The gaps that they leave behind can no longer be filled. You can admire them and you can build them monuments. Steve McQueen

Hand-made saddle, casual ape hanger bars, Wilbers suspension, and small mirrors and indicator. (Courtesy Yorck Dertinger)

Fuel tank with an elaborate glitter-star finish.
(Courtesy Yorck Dertinger)

Sucker Punch Sally's, United States

Founded in 2002, Sucker Punch Sally's focuses on stripped-down old school bobbers and choppers. Its 'Wild Child' custom take on Triumph's Thunderbird was shown at the Edmonton Motorcycle Show.

was such a legend, so was Dennis Hopper. With Dennis *Easy Rider* became a cult film – without this movie the world would be a little poorer. Hence we awarded this 1600cc cruiser a completely new style, as if the latest battleship of the British brand wouldn't have been designed for anything else. The performance of the twin hammer speaks for itself: 85hp and torque of 146Nm on tap from 2750rpm. There are people who claim they could hear quiet laughter in Dennis Hopper's final resting place in New Mexico. But this is how it is with such legends – they can always revive myths.

The Wild Child has a sprung seat, and rear-set foot pegs. The fuel tank and headlight have been given a vintage look, and the rear drive pulley (opposite) is spoked to match the rear wheel spokes: a nice touch.

Hinckley triples are no less customisable than their twin counterparts, as the bikes below demonstrate.

Steel Bent Customs, Florida, United States
Black Betty

Michael Mundy and his team began this project with a 1999 Triumph Adventurer, initially cleaning up its mid frame. Next, they built a new subframe to get a skinny rear, and hiked-up the seat, provided by Lance's Upholstery. Then they re-worked the electrics, hid the battery and wires, and fitted a custom three-into-one exhaust.

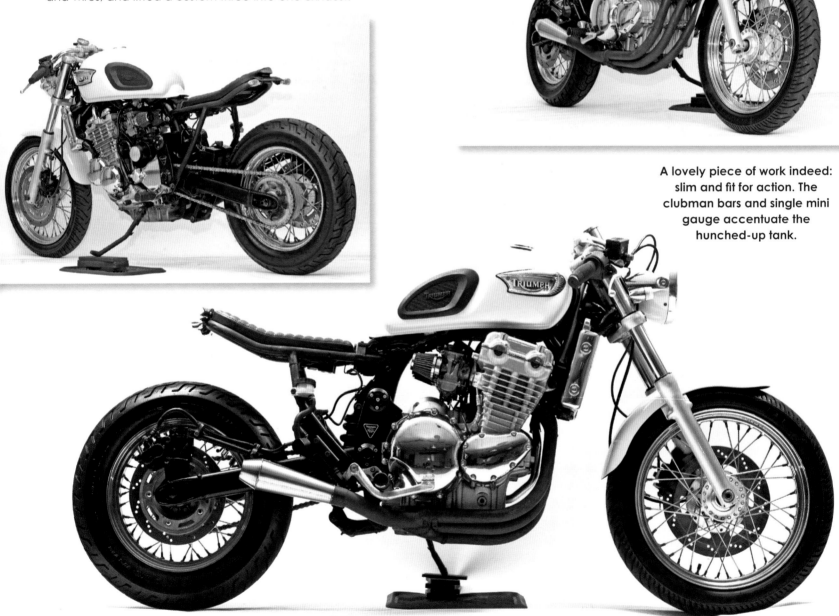

A lovely piece of work indeed: slim and fit for action. The clubman bars and single mini gauge accentuate the hunched-up tank.

The Triumph Rocket III is probably one of the hardest bikes to customise. This doesn't stop some people from giving it a go, though. Here are two examples:

DuSold DeSigns, United States

Mike DuSold and his team created a one-of-a-kind custom, built from the ground up, while retaining the factory Triumph fuel-injection and drivetrain. Everything else on this bike had to be fabricated. This motorcycle travelled the USA as the centrepiece of Triumph USA's show display at the time.

DuSold DeSigns provides high quality custom paint, airbrushing, metal fabrications and bodywork for cars, motorcycles, trucks, guitars, helmets, and more.

SPECIFICATIONS
Engine: 2300cc
Wheels: One-off Eggo Trip wheels, with 21in perimeter brake
Tyres: 360 rear
Suspension: Air suspension (Lays frame)
Throttle: Internal
Clutch: Internal
Manifold: Stainless race
Transmission: Billet jackshaft
Brakes: PM brake calipers
Air intake: Billet Velocity stacks
Radiator: Hidden
Frame: Hand-made
Fuel tank: Hand-made
Everything else: Hand-made

Roger Allmond Design, United Kingdom

Displayed at the 2008 NEC bike show in the UK, Roger Allmond's Triumph Rocket III concept bike was commissioned by Bennetts Insurance. Apart from using the 2.3-litre Triumph engine, fuel injection, wiring and shaft drive, all other similarities to the factory version stop there.

The Concept Rocket III sports an all hand-made aluminium frame, wheel hubs and spokes, and a single-sided tubular front suspension/steering setup. The carbon fibre wheel rims made by Dymag were the only externally sourced parts. Very nice indeed.

The Rocket Three Custom (which started life as a brand new 2005 Triumph Rocket III) on display at the 2011 Sydney Motorcycle Show. (Courtesy Mitch McPherson)

The project took Allmond six months to complete. (Courtesy Trevor Earl)

Hinckley Triumphs are increasingly seen in triking guise. A selection of such works can be seen here:

Mid Mo Mc, Mid-Missouri, United States

Mid Mo Mc is owned and operated by Norm Wilding, who hails originally from outside London, England. From a very early age, Norm was building hotrod motorcycles, taking Triumph engines and making them fit into Norton Featherbed frames, and building what is now known as the café racer style. In 1979, Norm built a Harley-Davidson 45 trike that took Best Engineering, Best Trike, and Best of Show at The Kent Bike Show, which was then (and still is) the most prestigious custom motorcycle show in Europe. Since then, he's been building quite a few more cool Harley trikes. Norm is the creator of this nice modern Triumph twin trike.

Norm's bobber-style Bonnie trike.

The Trike Shop UK, Cardiff, United Kingdom

The Trike Shop is a family-owned business that has been producing award winning trikes for the last 15 years. The team, fronted by Haydn and his wife Bev, have over 50 years of experience in the motorcycle industry. The business started in a garage at the back of Haydn and Bev's house, but Increased sales led to the purchase of a purpose-built unit on the outskirts of Cardiff.

The Trike Shop is also a dealer for Highway Hawk, Custom Chrome, Motorcycle Storehouse, Zodiac, Vance & Hines, etc, and can supply genuine Harley parts. Furthermore, the firm is expert in adaptations for the disabled rider, is a NABD Gold affiliated business, and is proud to

A Hinckley Thunderbird 900 retro model triked.

have had a long association with the National Association for Bikers with a Disability (NABD).

Triumph's Rocket III triple with its mighty 2300cc engine has become a popular choice for British trike enthusiasts. Here are three examples:

The silver Rocket III with twin headlights, ready to pounce.

A more conventional Rocket III with touring screen and pillion backrest.

The Rocket III Bug with custom exhaust and paint.

CHAPTER 5
Velocette-Vincent

VELOCETTE

Veloce Ltd was founded by John Taylor (previously known as Johannes Gütgemann) of Taylor, Gue Ltd, in 1905, in Birmingham. The first motorcycle produced was the Veloce. In 1913, the first two-stroke model was named Velocette. From then on, all subsequent models were Velocettes. The small, family-owned firm produced 250cc two-strokes from 1913-1925.

Velocette introduced an overhead camshaft (OHC) 350cc engine in 1925, leading to several roadster models developed from this so called 'K' series. This progressed to the KTT production racing model, built from 1928 to 1949.

In 1933, new overhead valve (OHV) machines were introduced, which led in 1935 to an entirely new model, the 500cc Velocette MSS, based on two previous OHV models.

The company gained an excellent reputation for its products, helped by two 350cc World Championship titles in 1949 and 1950. The 1954 Velocette MSS was popular with the US racing scene, heralding the development of Scrambler and Enduro versions of the model, and leading to the release of the 349cc Viper and 499cc Venom; both released in 1956. The late '60s saw the end of Velocette motorcycle manufacture, and Veloce Ltd finally closed its doors in 1971.

Mark Henning's Velocette, United States

Mark: "In 1970, a woman riding a horse told me that her husband had an old bike that started with a 'V' in a barn just up the road, and that I could have it. What she didn't tell me was that the barn had collapsed on it, but I dug it out and took it home anyway.

"The bike was in bad shape, most of the steel, including the tank and frame, was completely shot, so I gathered up parts that would work and made the rest."

Mark's custom started life as a 1963 Velocette MSS Scrambler.
(Courtesy Colin Seven)

Classic Moto Cycle, France

Pierre Jean (PJ) and Dominique (Dom) buy and sell antique, vintage and classic motorcycles, cars and collectibles from their Burgundy and Rhone Valley locations.

Pierre-Jean: "I bought this Velocette in a poor cosmetic state. The bike was converted for road racing in Scotland, thus it sports a tuned engine.

"As there was no lighting, a strange petrol tank and rear set, I decided to reassemble the racer as a bobber."

Velocette Venom 500cc 1961, bobber-style.
(Courtesy Pierre-Jean Gallet)

Since the author lives in New Zealand, he couldn't help but include NZ legend Bert Munro's Velocette racer.

Bert Munro, Invercargill, New Zealand

Abridged text courtesy of Maureen Bull, author of *New Zealand's Motorcycle Heritage*.

"Herbert James (Bert) Munro, (or Burt to the Americans), was born one of twins on 25 March 1899.

"His 1936 500cc MSS Velocette became the fastest recorded Velo. It was his mount for many an Oreti Beach race meeting between the 1950s and 1970s, and also his 1938 NZ GP ride on the custom circuit.

"Immortalised by the film *The Worlds Fastest Indian*, Bert is perhaps best remembered for his Munro Special, a 1920 Indian Scout which

Bert Munro's Velocette (red No. 5) on display at the E Hayes & Sons hardware store in Invercargill. (Courtesy Glen Bull)

became a work in progress from the time he acquired it until his passing.

Bert in 1975 on Oreti beach, Invercargill pointing to his 104th blow-up of the Velocette engine. (Courtesy Hayes Collection)

"Both his machines, when purchased, were standard road going models. The phenomenal speeds that he wrung from them was the result of his fertile brain, plus his single-mindedness – for the mind of the ordinary layman must have surely boggled at the task of rebuilding blown up motors and the hours of labour which Bert lavished on the Indian and the Velocette.

"Bert was an extremely able engineer whose Kiwi ingenuity got him out of many a tight spot and his charm won him mends and willing helpers during his action-packed lifetime on two wheels.

"To feature in New Zealand's motorcycle records over a period of four decades makes Bert Munro a dedicated speed merchant in anyone's terms. He set New Zealand records from 1940 to 1971.

"He survived countless crashes over the years and died in his sleep in Invercargill in January 1978, aged 78 years."

VINCENT

In 1928, Phil Vincent purchased the trademark and remaining components of HRD Motors Ltd (the JAP-powered motorcycle manufacturer was in financial difficulty at the time).

Shortly thereafter, the company was renamed Vincent HRD Co Ltd, and production moved to Stevenage. In 1949, the HRD in the name was dropped and superseded by the Vincent designation. Initially, JAP, Rudge-Python and Villiers engines were used. Phil Irving joined Vincent in 1931, and, by 1934, penned the OHV 500cc single cylinder Meteor. Next, Irving designed a V-twin, resulting in the Vincent HRD

Series A Rapide, introduced in late 1936. Irving decided to move on to Velocette in 1937, but returned to Vincent in 1943.

The Series B Rapide model, designed and introduced during the war, was very different from the A model. The cylinder angle was now 50 degrees instead of the 47.5 degrees of the Series A engine. This permitted the use of the engine as a stressed member of the frame, amongst other changes.

Girder forks with hydraulic damping distinguished the 1948 Series C Rapide from the Series B version. By 1950, the Rapide/Black Shadow produced between 45 to 55hp respectively, with the Black Shadow being capable of 125mph. The Black Lightning racer was substantially lightened by replacing many steel parts with aluminium. It was also fitted with a single racing seat and rear-set footrests. Vincent also built single-cylinder motorcycles, notably the 500cc Meteor and Comet singles, and the 500cc Grey Flash racer.

By 1954, declining sales caused Vincent more and more difficulties, and even a prototype three-wheeler didn't help matters. The company was forced to import and sell NSU mopeds to keep going, but sadly, by 1955, it was all over.

Redneck Engineering, United States

The name Vincent is generally associated with speed and racing, but how would the marque's glorious engine sit in a chopper-style bike? Well, judging by the looks of Mike Marquart's custom, it's looking pretty good indeed!

In 1976, the sight of a Vincent Black Shadow left quite an impression on Mike, and he has been taken with the brand ever since. A couple of years passed until he came across an estate sale of Vincent parts, centring around a 1951 998cc Vincent 'Series C' Black Shadow, with only the right timing case missing.

Close-up of the Vincent logo.

David Mann paintings in a VQ magazine provided the inspiration for the chopper's body design. Mike contacted Vince Doll from Redneck Engineering in Liberty, South Carolina, to do the work.

The entire build, welding, machining and parts fabrication was done by Redneck Engineering. The frame, mono shock, the motor as a stressed member, oval tubing and oil in backbone were Vince and Mike's ideas. Steve Hamel rebuilt the engine and ported the heads.

Special thanks to Steve Hamel, Weld Racing, Avon Tyres, and the crew at Redneck Engineering.

SPECIFICATIONS

Model: Vincent Black Shadow – 'Curves'
Owner: Mike Marquart
Frame: Mono-shock curved backbone using the engine as stressed member. 50-degree rake
Fuel tank: Custom, hand-made by Redneck
Rear mudguard: Custom, hand-made by Redneck
Front mudguard: NA
Handlebars: Redneck Engineering
Engine: 51 Vincent V-twin, 1000cc duel carb
Transmission: Vincent
Primary: Vincent
Exhaust: Redneck Engineering
Front wheel: Weld Forge Wire
Front tyre: 3.5 x 18, 150/70/18 Avon
Rear wheel: Weld Forge Wire
Rear tyre: 3.5 x 18, 150/70/18 Avon
Paint: Gary Strait, and graphics by Charlie Tyre

The front end consists of a tubular springer fork, custom-built to yield 4.00in trail. The frame tubing is elliptical and tapered for a sleeker design. The heat wrapped exhausts are hand-built by Redneck Engineering. The Weld Racing forged wire front and rear wheels are 18 x 3.5, with Avon 110/80-18 front and 150/70-18 rear tyres respectively. The fuel tank was hand-made by Vince Doll, and the Bonneville-style handlebars were also created by Redneck Engineering. (Courtesy Michael Lichter Photography)

CHAPTER 6

Japanese-built British customs

Japanese motorcycle culture developed a custom style all of its own, bringing forth a myriad of chopper and bobber conversions of Japanese marques. Some bike shops, however, have also produced customs powered by vintage British engines.

Kavach Motorcycles, Japan

Kazu Yamaguchi's shop is based in Tokyo, and produces customs powered by older Japanese or British engines. Kazu: "I opened my workshop fifteen years ago. All the engines of my bikes are fully rebuilt, and other needed parts are exchanged for new items. I also make my own exhaust pipes.

Regulations and registration about custom motorcycles are strict in Japan. I use frames of the 'Custom Rigid' type to pass the inspections."

SPECIFICATIONS
Engine: 1969 Norton Commando 750 (OHV-2)
Exhaust: Kavach
Transmission: Norton Commando 750
Forks: Norton Commando 750
Frame: Custom Rigid
Fuel tank: Kavach
Mudguards: Kavach
Seat: Kavach
Wheels: Norton Commando 750

Norton Commando, Kavach style. The peashooter pipes are a nod to standard Norton.

SPECIFICATIONS
Engine: 1979 Triumph T140V (OHV-2)
Exhaust: Kavach
Transmission: Triumph T140V
Forks: Kawasaki Z400GP (1982)
Frame: Custom Rigid
Fuel tank: Kavach
Mudguards: Kavach
Seat: Kavach
Wheels: Kawasaki Z400GP

A Triumph Bonneville after the Kavach treatment.

A selection of British engine-powered customs from a variety of Japanese custom shows:

Right: 1966 Triumph 650 made by Fork at the Yokohama Hot Rod Show – the tank and fender were sand cast. (Courtesy Kazuyoshi Janta Ueda)

Below: Kaikado-built Triumph custom, inspired by the Cushman Eagle. (Courtesy Motoyan)

Triumph chopper built by Kaikado outside the Joints Custom Bike Show in Nagoya. (Courtesy Motoyan)

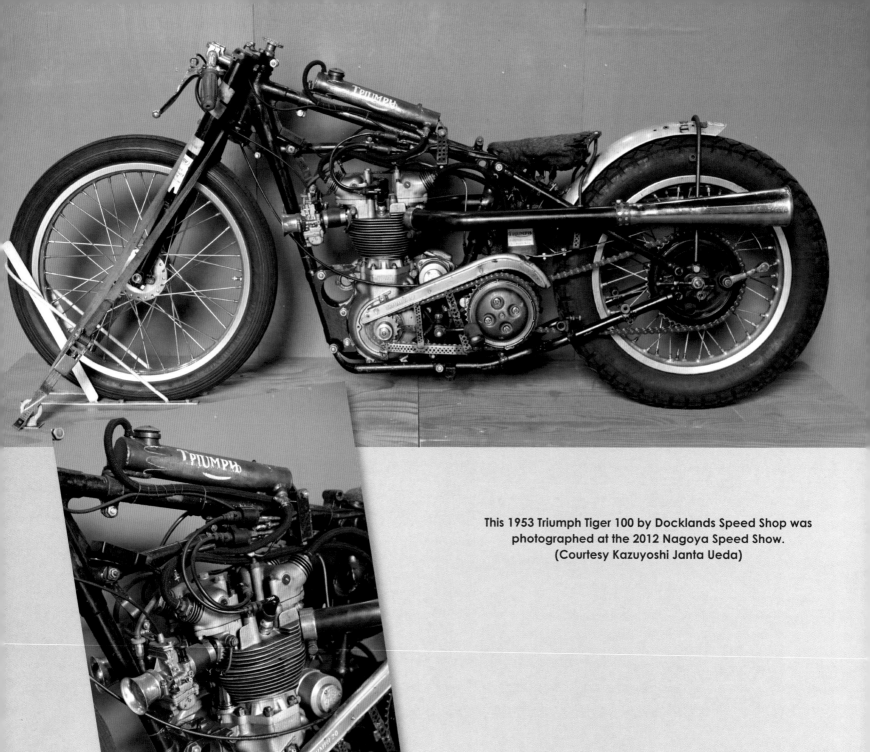

This 1953 Triumph Tiger 100 by Docklands Speed Shop was photographed at the 2012 Nagoya Speed Show.
(Courtesy Kazuyoshi Janta Ueda)

Opposite: A 1951 Vincent Rapide by Veronika at the Yokohama Hot Rod Show. Note the mesh style spokes on the front wheel.
(Courtesy Kazuyoshi Janta Ueda)

Royal Enfields are not spared the custom treatment in Japan either:

Stoop Motorcycles, Saitama

Although the shop concentrates on customizing Harleys, Stoop decided to go down the Royal Enfield route for a change. The more exposed Royal Enfield cylinder head – via the drastically altered fuel tank setup – and the hardtailed rear with humped seat, gives the bike a nice pose.

Heiwa Motorcycles, Hiroshima, Japan

Kengo Kimura launched Heiwa Motorcycles in 2005. His old-school custom design, applied to Japanese and British engines, combined with nice solutions to details, established Heiwa quickly in the custom scene. Kengo and his team accomplishes most tasks in-house, except for the paint-jobs. Heiwa means 'peace' in Japanese, hence the firm choosing to name some of its vintage British customs to reflect its name. The bikes shown here were all entrants in the annual Yokohama Hot Rod Custom Show.

AJS Green Peace
– built for the 2006
Yokohama show.
The engine is from an
AJS M16.

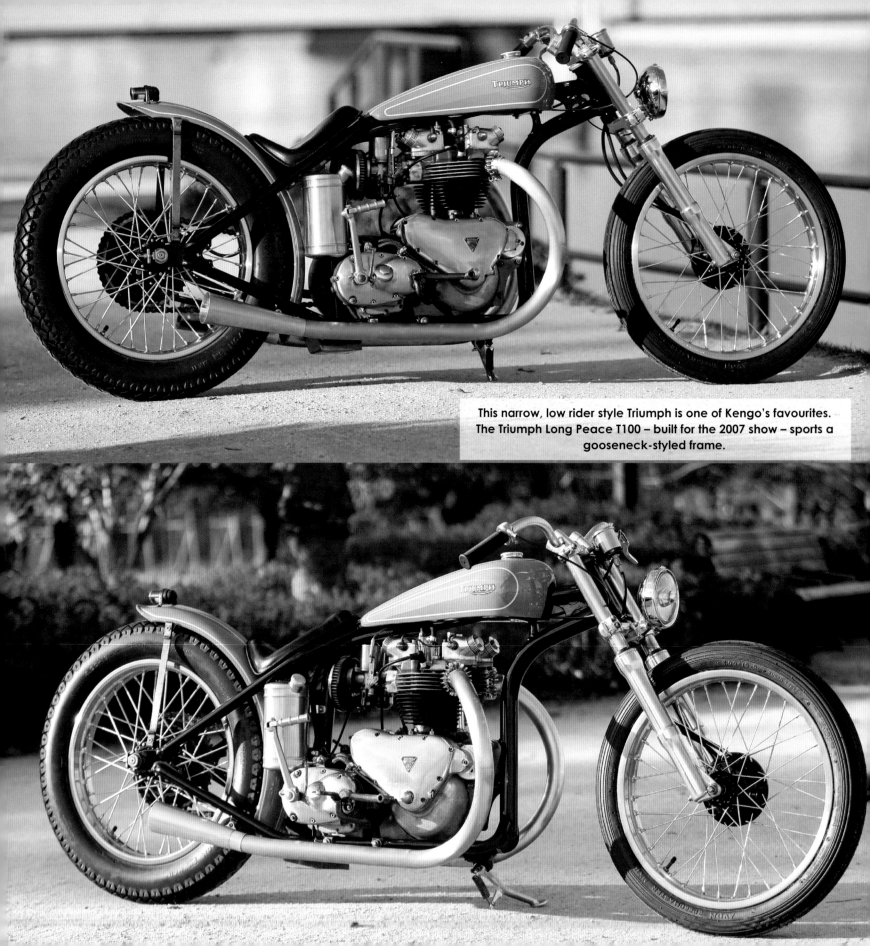

This narrow, low rider style Triumph is one of Kengo's favourites. The Triumph Long Peace T100 – built for the 2007 show – sports a gooseneck-styled frame.

The Matchless One Peace was built for the 2008 show. Heiwa favours a narrow and compact style. The bike features inverted forks, snaked exhaust, exposed sprockets, gooseneck frame, and typical Japanese custom tail light.

(And opposite): The Triumph Peaceful TR6 was built for the 2009 Yokohama Bike Show. It features Scrambler-style exhaust pipes, and a copper finish on the drive components.

The Norton Gentleman model 50 was built for the 2011 Yokohama show. It has lovely-looking architecture, with brass bolts and fasteners, and drilled fork covers.

CHAPTER 7
Indian-built Royal Enfield customs

Custom bike building is a fledgling industry in India, with a unique set of issues/difficulties, such as the lack of platforms to build bigger and better bikes, access to quality parts and accessories, etc. "You have to build everything to make a quality custom bike, which means fabrication, like sheet metal work, custom frames and swing-arms, machining of billet parts, custom painting, is all usually done in-house." (Jatinder Pal Singh)

Royal Enfield bikes in India are what Harley-Davidson stands for in the United States. The rest of India's bikerdom consists of millions of commuter bikes of various designations. The 350cc models are Royal Enfield's most popular choice in the domestic market, and are seen by many as most suited to Indian roads.

The firm's Bullet variants have been the biggest capacity bikes produced in the country for a long time, and are viewed by their followers as the Royal ride of choice.

It remains to be seen how brands like Harley-Davidson or Triumph will get on in the Indian motorcycle market.

Victory Customs, New Delhi

Jatinder Pal Singh: "Victory Customs started operations in November 2004 with dreams of creating customs which are totally unique to each owner. Every single bike should be a one-off, should have its own identity, look, feel and attitude. The bikes are made with just basic hand tools, a welding machine, and two power tools (4in grinder and hand drill machine). I am most thankful to my first customer, a dear friend, who believed in me and gave me an opportunity to build our first bike. Called Threat, it will always have a special place in my heart.

"We focus on building just six to eight bikes a year; quality before quantity is what we always believed in. We recently added some tools and benches for more efficiency, but we are still very much a small custom shop, building one custom at a time."

Panther / FX chopper

SPECIFICATIONS
Builder: Victory Customs
Engine: Single cylinder 350cc
Exhaust: Double-barrel one-off by Victory Customs
Transmission: Stock four-speed
Forks: Springer front end, custom-made by Victory Customs
Chassis: Stock modified by Victory Customs (stretched and raked to 40 degrees)
Dimensions: 8ft long
Suspension: Stock modified
Fuel tank: One-off by Victory Customs
Mudguards: None
Seat: Custom-made by Victory Customs
Wheels: Front, stock with 100-90-19 tyre, the rear was custom-made for a 150 rear tyre
Special features: Bike built in 60 days, and, apart from the stock engine, transmission and clutch, every single thing was custom-made. Chrome plating was outsourced, as was powder-coating. Painting was done in-house. The bike features no front brake, suicide shift, and a one-off fuel cap. The tail light was imported from the USA

The Panther ready to pounce.

Bulldog

The gas tank and exhaust are one-off
Victory Customs items.

SPECIFICATIONS:
Builder: Victory Customs, New Delhi
Engine: Single-cylinder 350cc
Transmission: Stock four-speed
Forks: Stock, modified with custom-made billet CNC-machined triple trees by Victory Customs
Chassis: Stock, modified by Victory Customs
Dimensions: Longer and lower than stock bike, nearly 7ft long
Suspension: Stock, modified
Mudguards: Custom hand-made steel mudguards by Victory Customs
Seat: Custom-made by Victory Customs
Wheels: Front, stock with 120 tyre, the rear was custom-made for a 150 rear tyre
Special features: Bike built in two months, and, apart from the stock engine, transmission and clutch, every single thing was custom-made. Chrome plating was outsourced, as was powder-coating. Painting was done in-house. The LED tail light was imported from the USA, and mated with a custom-made bracket

Victory Customs' first bike 'Threat.' The build took four months, from start to finish.

Cold sweat

SPECIFICATIONS
Builder: Victory Customs
Engine: Single cylinder 350cc
Exhaust: Stock, modified by Victory Customs
Transmission: Stock four-speed
Forks: Stock, modified, with custom-made billet CNC machined triple trees, by Victory Customs
Chassis: Stock, modified by Victory Customs (stretched and raked to 40 degrees)
Dimensions: 8ft long
Suspension: Stock, modified
Fuel tank: One-off by Victory Customs
Mudguards: Custom hand-made steel mudguards by Victory Customs
Seat: Custom-made by Victory Customs
Special features: Built in 75 days, and, apart from the stock engine, transmission and clutch, every single thing is custom-made. Chrome plating and powder-coating was outsourced. Painting was done in-house. The billet mirrors, tail light and fuel cap were imported from the USA

Cold Sweat's wheels feature Parado rims, with a 100-90-19 tyre on the front, and a 150 on the rear.

Seen at a Rider Mania event in 2012, conducted by Royal Beasters in New Delhi, this chopper features a fake rear cylinder.
(Courtesy Akshay Murthy)

Also on display at Rider Mania 2012, the builder of this extensively modified Royal Enfield is unknown. (Courtesy Deelip Menezes)

Please do Not Touch

Vardenchi Customs, Mumbai

Founded by Akshai Varde in 2005, Vardenchi sees its process of custom motorcycle building as a creative exchange between the company and the customer. Each Vardenchi is viewed as a work of art, rather than a combination of metal and wheels. Bikes are built to cater to the rider's individual needs, with stringent quality control to ensure each custom not only looks spectacular, but also rides with utmost quality. Vardenchi uses Royal Enfield as its base, but manufactures most of the custom parts in-house. Some items that can't be sourced locally, like wheels and tyres, are imported.

Vardenchi: "We offer end-to-end solutions in every area of custom motorcycle building, from sheet metal fabrication and structural fabrication, to an in-house painting and assembly unit. Our motorcycles are all about personality, attitude and looking great. A keen sense of design that arises from actually riding and experiencing the products on a day-to-day basis is the key. The entire process, from sketching the concept to 3D designing the parts and assemblies, and creating prototypes at every stage to checking for quality and fit and finish, makes a huge difference to the final product. The result is not just a motorcycle, but an extension of the rider's personality."

Vardenchi also manufactures bolt-on kits for Royal Enfields.

Vedic

SPECIFICATIONS
Foot control: Forward
Tank cap: Key cap
Front numberplate: Indi Mount
Indicator/tail light: LED
Speedometer: Digital LED Speedometer with nine different functions
Horn: 95mm diameter double disc horn.
Mirror: Classic chrome or powder-coated
Front brake: 260mm dia disc
Rear brake: 280mm dia disc
Handlebars: T-plate, handlebar on riser/single piece handlebar
Chassis: Raked, dropped saddle height, offset kit for drivetrain
Rake: 6in (Infinity) and 4.5in (Turbo)
Swingarm: Single-sided
Transmission: Belt drive
Front suspension: Telescopic
Rear suspension: Hidden double monoshock
Tyres: 130 x 17 front, 200 x 17 rear
Wheels: 17in alloy front, 17in offset alloy rear
Paint: Custom

(And opposite): The long and low Vedic chop features custom graphics and a semi free-flow exhaust.

The Dragster has custom wheels and a belt drive conversion, plus a mighty 300 x 18 rear tyre.

SPECIFICATIONS

Foot control: Forward
Tank cap: Key cap with embossed branding
Exhaust: Semi freeflow, short
Front numberplate: Indi Mount
Indicator/tail light: Tri Function LED
Speedometer: Digital LED Speedometer with nine different functions
Horn: 95mm diameter double disc horn
Mirror: Classic chrome or powder-coated
Brakes: 260mm diameter disc front, 280mm diameter disc rear
Handlebars: T-plate, handlebar on riser/single piece handlebar
Chassis: Raked, dropped saddle height, offset kit for drivetrain
Rake: 4.5in
Swingarm: Double-sided, twin-pipe, custom
Transmission: Belt drive
Suspension: Telescopic front, hidden double monoshock rear
Tyres: 100 x 21 front, 300 x 18 rear
Wheels: 21in-poke/alloy front, 18in-spoke/alloy rear
Paint: Custom

**Vardenchi's stretched out
Sunburn, with its custom wheels
and forward controls.**

Rajputana Customs, Jaipur

Rajputana's Vijay got his first motorcycle – a BSA Falcon/BSA Bond from his dad at the tender age of seven. A motocross course provided his training, coupled with racing in the 75cc class (against adults!). After studying in Ottawa, Canada, Vijay returned home to Jaipur in 2009.

After giving the matter some serious thought (and discussion with his family) Vijay decided to give his custom motorcycle building dreams a serious shot, and set up a garage in Jaipur. Rajputana Customs showcased its first bike 'Original Gangster' at the New Delhi Auto Expo in 2010. After a very positive response, and overwhelming affection for the bike at the expo, the firm began taking orders to build motorcycles for customers.

Vijay: "We strive to produce highly stylized, exquisitely detailed, awe-inspiring machines, with flawless functionality. So, if you have a bike and want to give it some individuality in the midst of the masses out there, then you've come to the right place. Be it modifications to an existing Royal Enfield, or having a custom bobber or chopper built from scratch ... we do it. Cause the machine that you sit on tells the world exactly where you stand."

The Nandi sports a 300mm rear tyre and a 23in front.

The Original Gangster's engine stems from a 350cc Royal Enfield. The bike features Springer fork suspension, a jockey shifter, internal throttle assembly.

SPECIFICATIONS
Wheels: Hubs machined from billet aluminium
Drive: Rear sprocket and jackshaft (secondary drive chain)
Suspension: Springer fork suspension
Engine: 500cc
Mirrors: Drop-down mirrors
Other: Brass ring highlights and etching, copper tubing to run the wiring for the rear tail lights

Sergey Egorov; Nepal
Himalayan Outlaw

Although modifications on motorcycles are strictly prohibited by government regulations, Sergey, nevertheless, built this Nepalese Royal Enfield bobber:

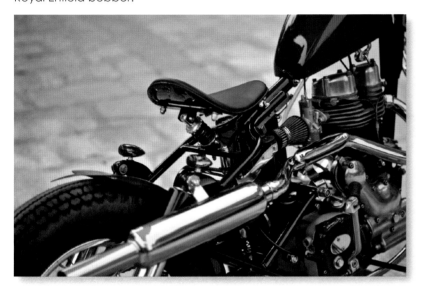

SPECIFICATIONS

Engine: 350cc/2006

Gearbox: Five-speed, left-side gear shift

Handlebars: Custom 1in black powder-coated drag bars, triple tree and risers

Swingarm/rear suspension: Custom-made swingarm, 5in longer than stock, vintage styled 13.5in UK-made gas shocks

Front brake: Stock hydraulic disc

Rear brake: Stock drum

Fuel tank: Harley-Sportster

Tyres: Avon Mk-II 130/90 tyre on 16in wheel rim

Seat: West-Eagle solo seat, suspension with hydraulic mini shock

Rear mudguard: Strutless, custom-made, 2mm blank steel

Stock Royal Enfield items: Fork tubes, front suspension, and front 18in wheel

Other: Crankcase breather box relocated and upgraded with K&N filter, gearbox cover-custom painted, custom-made stainless steel sump guard

The Outlaw has a Woodsman-style exhaust with heat shield fitted, and an Amal 26mm MkI concentric carb with S&B performance filter.

Index

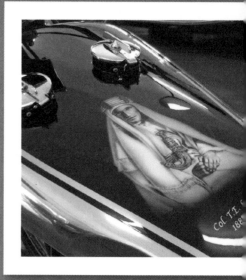